Crisis and the Miracle of Love

Through all the different ages of a human life there exist powerful catalytic or evolutionary points. In every culture, in every age, these power points have always been known and understood, but they are now ignored. The result has been the chaotic struggle each individual witnesses in their life today.

Tapping into these 'Miracle Points' we become free from destructive influences and self sabotage. This is a living guide book for life that no-one can really do without in our modern, hi-tech, fast-moving world where relationships are fragile and security tenuous.

We invite you to read this book and make the most important journey of your life.

© Dr Mansukh Patel & Dr Helena Waters 1997

First published in the United Kingdom in 1997 by
Life Foundation Publications
Maristowe House
Dover Street
Bilston
West Midlands WV14 6AL

ISBN 1 873606 11 7

Cover design and photography Regina Doerstel & Jeff Cushing
Illustrations by Nanna Coppens, Chris Ion & John Scard

Printed by Redwood Books, Kennet Way, Trowbridge, Wiltshire
Cover and colour plates by R.Weston (Printers) Ltd, Dixon St., Wolverhampton, W. Midlands

Crisis & the Miracle of Love

Mastering Change and Adversity at any Age

Dr Mansukh Patel and Dr Helena Waters

Life Foundation Publications

Crisis and the Miracle of Love
is dedicated to all you special people who have
supported Eurowalk 2000. Thank you for your help in
organising seminars, giving food and shelter and for your generous
gifts to people in need. May this book help you, your children
and all future generations to come.

Contents

Chapter

It has been a refreshing experience to read this book, and to explore the thoughts of two very experienced people who have given of their time, interest and understanding to help present-day society's problems.
In a time full of confusion, economic battles and unemployment, when we sometimes appear to have to fight for our own existence, this book comes as a breath of fresh air.

The methods, thoughts, exercises, meditations and thought-provoking stories from rich, famous and man in the street alike, all combine to make this a book of inestimable value. We all need guidance in life, without a doubt, and as Martin Luther King said so well, 'The ultimate measure of a man is not where he stands in moments of comfort and convenience, but where he stands in times of challenge and controversy.'

Not only is this a book about love, it is also about faith in life and it is a book which will have a long future because it addresses the most vital issues about life in all its myriad forms.

I so often quote in my lectures that man has not just one body but three - physical, mental and emotional - and these have to be brought into harmony in order to experience the good health and positive love for life which are our birthright. As a practitioner of almost forty years, originally trained in the orthodox field of medicine but having spent most of my life in alternative medicine, books like this one are of enormous help to me and fill a tremendous gap.

A lot of the advice and thoughts come from grass root level wisdom - something that we have lost. They have given me a lot of food for thought and I personally feel that I would like everyone to delve into their wisdom, love and understanding. May this book be a blessing to the many people who have been waiting for it.

Jan de Vries - author and broadcaster
D.Ho.med. D.O.M.R.O., N.D.M.R.N., D.Ac., M.B. Ac.A

Miracles happen in the presence of love.

Nothing stirred on the plains except the slow moving herds of elephants and gazelles. Far off in the distance, Mount Kilimanjaro rose majestically out of the Great Rift Valley. Enveloped in a shimmering haze, it appeared as still as the Masai warrior standing on one leg, motionless as a watchful crane gazing at some distant horizon.

A momentary breeze rippled through the long grass bringing welcome relief from the intensity of the East African sun. The great lioness, sleek and powerful, stretched out across the branch of the low-hanging tree where she lay resting in peaceful languor. Nothing stirred, everything so silent and still.......

As we came running through the long grass, sleepy snakes slithered from our path in all directions eager to escape the human stampede. Colourful birds rose up from the ground shrieking in alarm as our laughter filled the air with the excitement of four friends looking for adventure.

The sleeping lioness half opened her eyes, disturbed by our approach, half interested, half not. She closed them again, drifting back into a lazy sleep.....

We were looking for fun, catapults at the ready to hit any target. How could we have known it was a lioness? Before we knew what had happened we were running - running for our lives and moving faster than we had ever moved before. Running like the wind, we hardly noticed the long grass cutting into our legs and slashing our thighs as we sped towards the Masai village - and safety.

My legs were moving faster than I had ever dreamed possible - as another almost unearthly force seemed to take them over. What force was propelling them? Fired by a terror I had never felt before I had to keep running, running, running...I was being chased by a lioness - I kept running.

It was the first crisis of my young life and one that taught me many things. That night, as I sat round the fire with my father, he instructed me. 'You must never run away, Manu,' he said. 'Always face adversity head on. If you run away from a wild cat it will inevitably get you because they can run at over sixty miles an hour and you...' He laughed as he thought about the possibilities of a young seven year old boy out-running a lioness. 'You were lucky.' And then, shaking his head from side to side, he added quietly, 'It was a miracle.'

I always remember his words and the power of his message to me whenever I find myself confronted by adversity. He wasn't just talking about how to deal with the wild animals of Africa, but the way I should face my whole life. He was telling me to move through every experience with courage and fearlessness and to look for the miracles...to go into its power and possibilities. Crisis comes as a means of breaking barriers that prevent us from experiencing more profound aspects of who we really are. Crisis is a gift that can take us into deeper and deeper love - if we let it.

Something woke up inside me that day and it has always stayed with me. What was the power that came into me? What was that sheer force of energy that I never even knew that I had that showed me how to run at such incredible speed? Where did it come from and could I find it again?

Since that time I have faced many more dangers, each time discovering the same vast reservoir of power and energy. It never fails me so long as I live by his words and turn to face whatever life is presenting me with. Then, as the impossible becomes possible, life's intricate pattern reveals itself to me a little more clearly. Slowly and surely, every incident has helped me to understand the power of my life. I invite you to look at your own life and to transform every crisis into a miracle of love.

- Mansukh

You cannot cross the ocean by merely staring at the water.

- Tagore

My elder daughter told me of her first experience of Antarctica as a marine biologist. She fell in love with the penguins, but couldn't believe the apparent cruelty of the parents who just walked out on the chicks, leaving them to fend for themselves. Over the following few days she watched fascinated as the braver chicks ventured out of the nest in search of food, and found themselves teetering on the edge of a cliff towering above frigid ice-strewn waters.

Even the hunger they felt could not entice them to take the plunge into the crashing waves below. Reassured that death from starvation was preferable to a death on the rocks they made their way back to the safety of the flock. But one penguin didn't really believe it..., so being a 'great' penguin, he went quietly back to the edge, and made the decision to 'go for it'. He closed his eyes, and bravely leapt into the unknown. He disappeared for a moment in the inhospitable waves. Seconds later, to his own delight, he re-emerged, churning his wings with glee. 'I did it! I did it!' He called to the others, 'Come on in, it's great. This is how it is meant to be. This is what we are supposed to do.'

In life, as with the penguins, only a brave few follow this example. It takes courage to take a leap into the unknown.

I met Mansukh ten years ago. To him I am very grateful. It was one of the most precious moments I can remember. Here was a man who had launched himself into the great sea of life. Since that time I have discovered beyond a doubt that the source of all our strength lies within us. It is just waiting to be acknowledged.

Crisis gives us the opportunity to tap into the power of the unknown. Crisis and adversity are the keys to discovering the purest element within ourselves, and without them we can remain 'asleep', and even oblivious to life. Life is wanting to wake us up! At every age we are given opportunities to do so - to wake up to the truth of who we are and what we are capable of.

So many of us are faced with the plight of living in a Western scientific civilisation that has lost touch with the heart of humanity. Modern life has become fraught and full of stress and anxiety, bereft of the inherent power and stillness one can sense in the native cultures.

I have been a child, a mother and grandmother, wife and teacher, doctor and psychiatrist. All my experiences have taught me one thing. I, like you, am only a student of life. We are on this exhilarating journey together - a journey of awakening from the first in-breath to the last out-breath. Thank you for taking up the challenge. I offer you this book as a gift - an invaluable companion and a trusty guide.

*- **Helena***

CHILDHOOD AND PARENTING

Share with the children
that hope springs eternal
and to love themselves
and see themselves as worthy,
that they came here by choice,
not by accident. ....
.....As a result of that choice,
parents have a responsibility
and that is to set the best example.

- The Wisdom of Little Crow

It is late at night. A Bushman mother is standing under the Kalahari desert sky holding her child high above her head towards the stars. She is praying to the stars on behalf of her baby that each one of them will offer a part of their light to guide its journey through life.

In offering her child to the universe in this way, she is creating a relationship for the child between itself and the world it has come into.

That relationship will provide a foundation that will endure for the whole of its life.

Radha Patel - Mansukh's daughter

I have many flowers, but the children are the most beautiful flowers of all.

- Oscar Wilde

4

*A*s a boy growing up in Kenya, I noticed that the Masai women always carried their children on their backs for the first two years. The indigenous cultures instinctively know and understand that this is the crucial bonding time between a mother and her child.

Some tribes will not allow their children to even touch the ground for the first nine months of their life and the deep significance of this cannot be underestimated in the unfolding emotional awakening of the child. The message of the mother, the only meaningful focus of the child's life is, **'I am completely here for you.'**

The power of that commitment means that they grow up emotionally stable and secure, strong and confident that life is something to be trusted. In our modern civilised society, a mother often finds herself deprived of the time-honoured and ancient skills so essential for the awesome task of raising children.

What can we offer to our children that will give them the firm foundation they need?

They deserve the very best that we can give them and *we* deserve an essential tool kit of parental guidance!

The insights in this chapter contain the power of centuries of tried and tested parenting skills, passed on from my own mother who, although unable to read or write, remained true to the ancient tradition into which she was born.

- Mansukh

In the beginning ...

At last! The room is ready, carpeted and wall-papered. The cot looks magnificent with its gorgeous matching quilt and pillows. You have had the 'seal of approval' from all the friends and relatives ... all you need now ... is the baby!

You have probably read all the books and magazines and listened to all the good advice in the world. You feel excited and maybe a little uncertain as you wait for the magical moment when the real job of parenting will begin.

Weeks of intensive parenting, however, can leave us feeling quite different from the text-book images....

People who say they sleep like a baby usually don't have one!

- Leo Burke

The crisis of parenting

Nobody ever told me it was going to be like this! Where's my freedom
gone? How am I going to cope? I can't be totally responsible for this
other life, can I? I feel inadequate, incapable, overwhelmed and, quite
honestly ... scared!

Yes, it takes a while to adjust to all the changes that a baby brings but
luckily things settle down after a while as we become more relaxed and
confident.

There is a growing realisation, however, and an uneasy feeling that this
little person has come to stay! I am now totally responsible for
maintaining its life, health and future development. Help! Nobody has
ever told me how to do it!

Children are our teachers

What do I tell them? Teach them? Show them? What do they really need? Amidst the initial turmoil of this process of self-questioning there also exists an atmosphere of the magical and the miraculous which can become an awakening experience. Why? Because children offer us the opportunity to live at the very heart of life itself.

Helena and her granddaughter Gaia

The most important thing to realise about being a parent is that our children have come to teach us things we have forgotten. It is not so much about teaching them as **learning from them,** because they know a lot more about being happy and enjoying life than we do! They can even help us to stay healthy, young and full of fun.

10

Have you noticed how children are always laughing? Sometimes they don't even need anything to laugh at. They just do it because it feels good!

They respond to life in a completely spontaneous way, unhindered by having to analyse or 'work things out'.

They are fascinated by life and full of wonder at the simplest things - the rainbow colours of a bubble, for instance, and the way it explodes into nothingness.

When was the last time you got excited about a bubble?

Children give us the opportunity to remember and become re-acquainted with the magic of our own childhood. If we let them, they will take us back into their world, where life is simple and wonderful.

Some Natural Laws of Parenting

1 *Unconditional love*

Children need to be supported unconditionally through all the changes they will experience if they are to develop the inner tools which make it possible to gain a clear picture of their true goal in life.

So often a child's life can be governed by fear and threats of, 'If you don't behave in the way I feel is appropriate, I will withdraw my love.' Unconditional love asks us to make our children feel that we will always love them no matter what.

Approaching children in this way we benefit just as much as they do...

A moment of pure love

One evening, my twelve year old son and I were busy brushing our teeth. 'Aha!' I was thinking, 'the perfect opportunity to sort out the few acts of mischief I have been informed of.' He had found a box of water pistols stored in the barn for our special 'Pathfinder' courses and had not been able to resist breaking it open and 'borrowing' one of them. I was ready for a show-down!

I knew that this and a few other issues I needed to talk about could leave us both feeling bruised and hurt. Was it going to be another one of those 'don't do it again or else' talks?

This time I wanted to appeal to his youthful, yet very capable sense of reasoning and a deeper feeling of care towards the things that he engaged in during the day. Was he ready to go a step further in his feelings? Would he think about the consequences of his actions and have a sense of value for how those actions might affect others?

13

Not only that, was I willing to take a step further in treating him with the respect and reverence he deserved? As I probed into the day's events it became clear that we were involved in a battle of wills.

Suddenly I stopped. 'You know,' I said to him, slowly and carefully choosing my words. His little ears were buzzing with anticipation. 'You really mean a lot to me and I want you to know that I will always love you no matter what you do.' Everything went very quiet between us. He was watching the tears trickling down my cheeks. He had never seen his Dad cry before. 'But you know,' I continued, 'if I am to achieve what I need to, I really need your help.'

He looked at me with wide, incredulous eyes which were also filling with tears. 'Come here and give me a hug,' I said, and as the sun set over the valley we stood together in the bathroom holding on to each other and our toothbrushes, our mouths still full of toothpaste!

Arjuna Patel - Mansukh's son

It was the start of a new relationship and a new direction in our lives together. All the old judgement and condemnation of the past disappeared in one pure moment of unconditional love.

- Mansukh

15

2 *Quality time and bonding*

Taking time to really 'be with' our children

Any moment can become magical if we are willing to stop our 'busyness' and to spend time with our children. If we want to create a bond with them it is essential always to make time for quality interactions. It will give them a deep sense of security and a feeling of being loved and valued.

Children will grow up slowly if we have made time for them, otherwise they will be grown up and gone before we know it.

You can always tell a family that makes time for bonding because they emanate a strength and fun-filled understanding amongst themselves that outsiders can only admire.

Action plan

◆ **Play together** - but preferably not competitive games that can create arguments! Games like frisbee, football and tig bring a sense of fun-filled laughter into your relationship.

◆ **Sit together** - reading stories is one of the most precious ways to connect and bond with our children at a deep level.

◆ **Eat together** - never underestimate the importance of eating together as a family. Make it a time to look forward to, full of discussion and happy interactions.

Whatever you do with your children make sure it involves inter-action and not distraction. Television can create de-bonding unless you watch things that make you laugh together or programmes like 'Mastermind' where you can all be involved together.

The most exciting moment

'Do you know what the most incredible moment of my life was, Bapu?' my youngest son said to me one day. 'No, tell me,' I replied, sensing that he was about to say something very important.

'When I was small (he is quite small now!) I used to sit at the bottom of the stairs waiting for someone to tie my shoe laces and sometimes I had to wait a long time. One day, while I was waiting I tried to do it myself and it just happened by accident!' he said excitedly. 'I ran into the room to tell everyone shouting, "I've just tied my shoe lace!" but nobody seemed as excited as I was.' 'Why do you think that was, Krishna?' I asked him. 'They were all too busy,' he said matter-of-factly.

'How sad,' I thought, 'that we are too busy to notice the most exciting moment of a little boy's life.'

- Mansukh

19

3 *Listening*

How much time do we really take to listen to what our children are trying to communicate? Children really value being heard and respected for what they have to share. If they are, they will grow up strong and confident about who they are, free from self-doubt and inadequacy.

One mother we know used to ask her children every night, 'What was the most unpleasant thing that happened to you today?' followed by, 'What was the most pleasant?' One day her youngest daughter replied to the first question, 'Mummy, you didn't listen to me properly!' Imagine her feeling when a few days later her daughter's best thing from the day was, 'You really listened to me today.'

You will notice that as you actively engage in listening to your children, their ability to listen to *you* will magically improve. Try it and see!

Action plan

✓ Take time to listen to their first thoughts of the morning. It may be dreams, or yesterday's events. It may be their concerns for the day at school. Enter into *their* dialogue and, if necessary, *create* it for them.

✓ When you are driving in the car, use the opportunity to ask questions and really listen to what they have to say.

✓ Spontaneous outbursts from a child contain the most precious moments. **Be there for those moments.**

✓ As soon as they come back from school, take time to be interested in what they have to share about their day.

4 *The power of our command words*

Do you remember the last time someone said 'NO!' to you? How did it feel? Amplify that ten times and that is how your children feel, because they are much more sensitive.

The word 'No' may create 'convenient' behaviour, but perhaps at the expense of our children's real feelings and integrity. One of the easiest ways to destroy children in fact, is to make them feel that we know more than they do. Children are individuals and no matter how much we *think* we know, the way they will express themselves in life is going to be totally unique.

> *...as the snail whose tender horns being touched,*
> *shrinks back into its shelly cave,*
> *with pain long after fearing forth to creep again.*
>
> *- William Shakespeare*

Scan these statements and see if you recognise any you use

'You can't do that!'
'You always make a mess!'
'You never clear away your toys!'
'You stupid boy/girl - you are so...disgusting.'
'You little devil...'

See how many negative labels you put on your children as you react to situations that arise around you daily. Make a list of empowering things you could say and make a commitment to use them more often.

◆ Recognise that our negative statements most often arise out of irritation, impatience and frustration at having to deal with repetitive situations we feel are out of our control.

◆ Become aware of how many times you say 'No' to your children. If necessary, rearrange things so that they are not inhibited by your needs.

23

◆ If you want to know if your command words are working or not, observe the expression on their faces when you tell them something and watch their body language. You may need to adjust the tone of your voice, or touch them before you say anything.

◆ Take a moment to understand your children's perspective. It will often differ from yours. For example, their mess is not a mess to them! In fact, 'messy' is a question of perception. It's very unlikely that a child will see it in the same way as an adult.

◆ Have an appreciation of their right to be 'right' although you feel wholly justified with your own viewpoint. **They feel the same.**

◆ It's important to remember that young children are rarely 'wrong' as such. **Their actions are either convenient to us or not.** Are we trying to fit their free-flowing spirits into our needs and adult sense of values?

Children will not remember you for the material things you provided but for the feeling that you cherished them. - *Robert L. Evans*

5 *The crucial balance of give and take*

From 2 - 5 years old children must have the freedom and space to explore fully. It is important not to inhibit children's needs to express themselves and to create a safe environment for exploration. There are obvious moments when we must lay down the law, but it needs to be finely balanced against their natural inheritance for self expression.

They need to learn about their relationship with the world and will arrange things in a room so that they can find their own place in it. They are learning about colours, distance and size and will pick up a ball and throw it in their exploration and need to learn about spatial arrangement. How far does the ball go? What about a cube?

So the 'mess' they create is a perfectly ordered arrangement to them. Isn't it beautiful?

Action plan

✓ Did you know that everything that happens as a mental stimulus on the outside gets conditioned into our nervous system? We live in a hi-tech stimulating society and too much exposure to TV, videos and computer games can leave children growing up without ever discovering themselves. Try to minimise these activities and turn them towards a more natural life.

✓ Create a damage-proof creative environment for young children to feel free to explore and enjoy. (A home filled with Grandma's antique furniture and crockery is an ideal stress-inducer!)

✓ Avoid taking them to places where their need for exploration will clash with your need to get something done - like supermarkets!

6 *Guiding with respect for their uniqueness*

The perfect balance

Children need to be guided and if you carry this out with love, strength and firmness, it will leave them feeling inwardly empowered and supported even though outwardly a little grumpy!

Between the ages of 2 and 5 they have an extraordinary ability to absorb new information and ideas and record over a thousand new impressions and experiences every day. We have to be very careful not to dampen it all down by influencing them on how to experience the world. It can destroy their confidence in the way they perceive life.

In fact, isn't that what happened to us? And as a result we suffer today from our inability to trust our decisions and to be excited and passionate about events in life.

Action plan

✓ Set reasonable and sensible limits.

✓ The emotional energy with which you implement a decision, either for or against something is what is important. It is this energy that children will learn to adopt and relate to when family situations of a similar kind arise in his or her adult life.

✓ The most successful parents we have met have been those who use the power and strength of **genuine love** for all their interactions.

✓ Sandwich setting boundaries and limits with fun and laughter. Someone we know always puts on a Donald Duck mask and a funny voice to say things like, 'Shall we tidy up now children?'

Resolving the Rift of Tension

If they are honest with themselves, many parents develop an ever-widening sense of isolation from their children as they begin to assert themselves as individuals. This can lead to the gradual breakdown of parent/child communication.

I just can't understand my children - they never listen to me!
But if we want to understand someone - don't we have to listen to *them?*

But I'm at the end of my tether!
Sound familiar? When agitation between you and your children has become chronic you will have to stop and make space to look at the situation objectively. However far you have to go to find your part in the situation - find it!

 Your children deserve this.

31

Emergency 5-point action plan

✓ Before reacting verbally, mentally or physically, Stop! Run into the bathroom and take this book with you to remind yourself what to do next!

✓ Take a few moments to step back and look at the whole scene objectively.

✓ Close your eyes. Sit comfortably, straighten your back and inhale deeply through the nose. Take one deep breath, hold for three seconds and exhale calmly to the count of five. Repeat three times. Repeat the same breath three more times using the affirmation, 'I have the power to resolve this.'

✓ Take responsibility for your part in it. What are your children mirroring in you?

✓ Ask yourself: Will the outcome that I desire benefit both of us or only me? What is the best outcome so that both of us can win? Pause and wait for creative answers. Your mind has the capacity to give you a solution to any questions you have to ask. Once you have some clear ideas go out and take appropriate action.

In the event that you cannot come up with any solution, stay neutral because win-win and nobody wins are just as good as each other. Stay in the bathroom and have a shower!

 Remember to focus 10% on the problem and 90% on solutions.

Possible causes of disruptive behaviour:

Home influences
1. Sleep patterns. Are they going to bed too late?
2. Are they watching too much television and what are they watching?
3. Are you giving them space to be with you in a loving way? Remember how much they need this bonding time.

Diet
What kind of food are they eating? Is it high in sugar which creates hyperactivity? If so, change their diet! Are they allergic to something? Are they eating last thing at night? If so, encourage them not to.

Outside influences
1. What kind of company are they keeping?
2. What is happening at school?
3. Is their creativity finding a satisfactory outlet?

Children as a mirror

The uncomfortable truth is that our children mirror two things - what they learn at home and what they learn at school. If we want their behaviour to change, we are going to have to spend more time with them! We need to think of ourselves as evolving, growing, human beings and not just parents who have 'children to look after'. It's a two-way process and in any given situation that is causing stress **no one party is completely to blame.**

✓ Try to open to a spontaneous perspective. Each moment and interaction makes a difference and every day is a new day for growth.

✓ Visualise your children as fully grown adults to help you gain a perspective of who they really are.

A parent learns by making mistakes!

Almost as soon as a pilot takes off from the runway the plane is off course and he will often have to do a complete circle to get it back again. Within fifteen seconds the plane will be off course again and so the pilot's job is to constantly counteract the tendency until he lands the plane. This is what parenting is like! We are always veering 'off course' and just need to adjust things on a constant basis. You are both learning. 'Firmness' is born of care, concern and love. 'Force' is a different thing altogether.

Action plan

✓ Try keeping a 'Kid's Diary' and write down any 'mistakes' you may have made during the day.

✓ It helps you to remember them and to re-assess your parenting skills.

✓ You could pass it on to your children when they are older to help them to learn parenting.

✓ **Look back on the day**

What could you have said or done that might have made your relationship with your children more harmonious?

✓ **Admit** to yourself that you may have done the wrong thing.

✓ **Forgive** yourself.

✓ **Congratulate** yourself for the times when you got it right!

✓ Try to release any guilt feelings from the day's interactions. If something happened that you believe is your 'fault' - let it go, because your children already have. Unavoidable incidents will often give your child the ability to be more balanced, alert and awake.

✓ Resolve hurts from the day. It's fine to say 'sorry' because it will heal your relationship.

Do you ever take a quiet look at your children as they are sleeping? In those precious moments we may wonder who are these little people who have been entrusted to our care for so many full and adventurous years to come.

Ancient traditions see a star-studded night sky as being filled with the countless wise and guiding saints and a falling star represents a wise being returning to the earth.

If we look at our children, we will see that they have something there that we may have lost. Perhaps they have come to remind us of that starlight within us and to open our hearts once again to the wonder and the beauty of life.

Certainly they have come to teach us something very profound. May we discover this great truth for ourselves.

The Teenage Years

Welcome to the Turbulent Teens!

*Y*ou have to be inside a teenage body to really understand what it's like.

If you are watching the teens from the outside - as a parent or teacher, for example - you will probably find it almost impossible to remember how wild it was amidst the swings and storms of your changing body and emotions.

And if you are on the inside - somewhere between twelve and twenty - you are probably wishing you knew what was going on and that you had somewhere to stand where you could just relax and be yourself.

What is the crisis of the teens all about?

It's all about 'self' consciousness and a desperate search for your own identity. You start to feel an ever-increasing need to break away from the restrictions of childhood and to be independent and recognised as someone with your own thoughts and feelings.

As your body starts to change and grow, something deep inside is urging you to discover yourself. You are trying to become 'someone' and be recognised in your own right. You are putting on the clothes of individuality and self-expression.

In fact the games that boys and girls play with each other will start to dominate your heart and mind. 'Will he/she like me?' 'Am I attractive enough?' 'Why does he like her/him? - what's wrong with me?' All these and many more emotions start to rage inside and take over. It can be very painful as you assess yourself through other people's eyes and try so hard to be what you think they will find acceptable.

As you start to compare yourself with others it can make you feel a bit insecure and uncertain. 'Shouldn't I be thinner or fatter or better-looking?' 'I wish I was as clever as ... or had nicer clothes.'

Sometimes it can seem that everyone has better qualities than you and self-esteem can become a **big** issue. It's easy to feel that your image is not quite 'cool' enough.

What's happening to me?

Nothing is the same inside from one day to the next. When you ask, 'How do I feel?' I don't know because every day is different. My emotions aren't anywhere - they are all over the place!

What I love is to just be me. You know? To explore and find out about everything. It's no good having someone else tell you something. You only understand it if you experience it for yourself. So that's what I am doing now. I wish everyone would let me get on with it.

- Michelle 14

Once the hormonal changes begin, you will become painfully aware of your body and how happy or unhappy you feel about it. Suddenly 'boys' and 'girls' take on a whole new meaning! Natural attraction is taking place. You start to feel an urgency about being attractive and desirable which can give rise to a whole range of confusing emotions.....

I'd just had my hair cut and, horror of horrors, it looked terrible! I couldn't bear anyone else to see me so there I was sitting in this party with my baseball cap on.

'Why are you wearing that hat?' my friend asked me.

'Because I have had the most terrible haircut and I look awful,' I replied miserably.

She looked really surprised and said, 'Hey! You are so much more than a hair cut!'

I felt as though I had been set free! She was right! I realised that people just don't think about me the way I think they do. I also realised what a great friend I had.

- Susan 17

The only answer in fact, is to decide to feel good about who you are, no matter what shape or size you are or what you look like.

Feeling great about yourself doesn't just happen though. It's something **you really have to work at** just like maths and biology or training for football.

It is really worth the effort because when you feel great about yourself, everyone will feel great about you.

 This is the secret of the universe by the way!

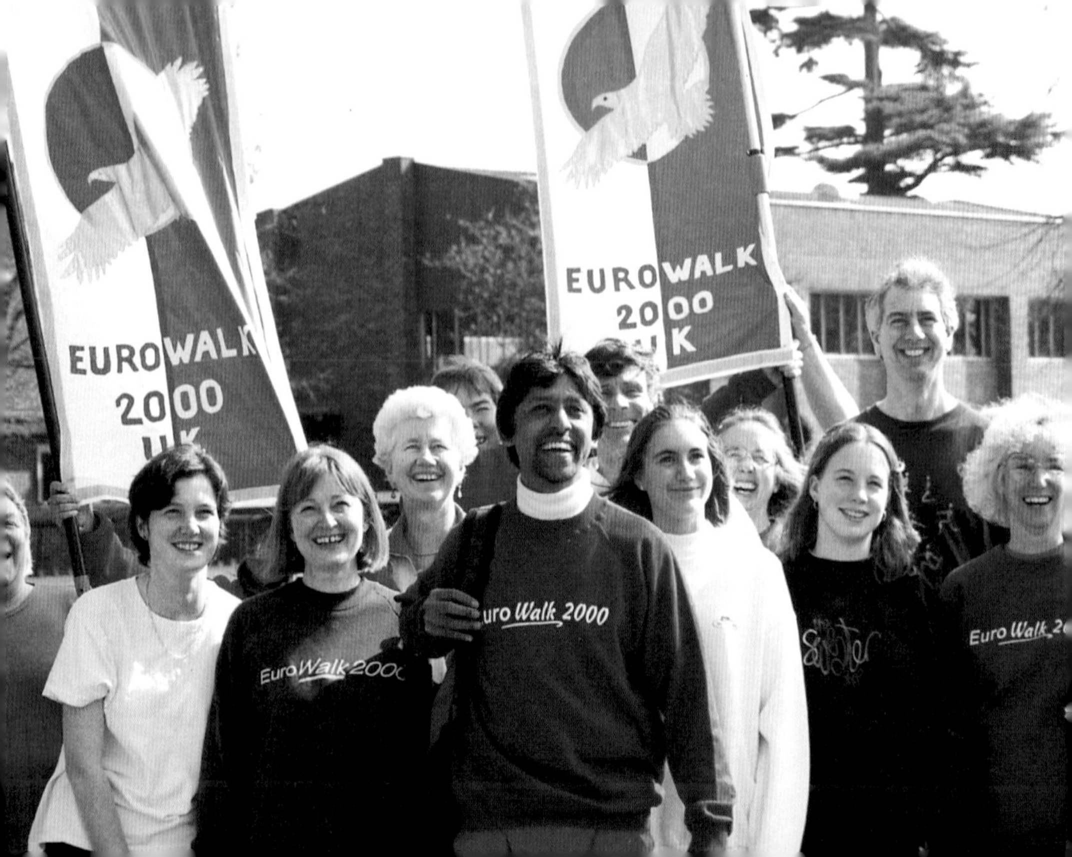
EUROWALK
2000
UK
EUROWALK
2000
Euro Walk 2000

A Five Point Plan for the Teenage Years

1 Establish yourself -
become rooted in who you are

When everything feels unstable and fluctuating, this posture will help to stabilise your energy. Feeling grounded and secure, you will feel established in who you are.

The Tree Posture

Stand up straight. Take hold of the right foot and place it high on the inside of the left thigh. Breathe in and slowly raise the arms above the head. Press palms together and hold this posture for 15 seconds. Fix your eyes on a still point in front of you to help you to keep your balance.

Repeat on the other side.

51

2 Look after your health

Be happy with your body and accept it as it is.

The way you feel is directly connected to the food you eat and how much you exercise your body, because the mind and body are inextricably linked.

Have you ever noticed that when you are physically active and feel healthy you tend to feel better about yourself?

Try to eat a healthy, balanced diet containing minimum amounts of sugar and junk foods which can cause depression and moodiness (and spots!)

Regular exercise will keep you feeling happy and healthy and less prey to negative thoughts.

Conquest of thoughts is more difficult
than the conquest of the world
through force of arms.
Conquer your thoughts
and you will conquer the world.

- *Sivananda*

3 Directing energy creatively

Negative thought storms

Everybody goes through it! You feel caught up in a voice inside your head which says,

'I'm no good,' or 'I'm all alone, nobody understands me,' or 'I'll never be able to do that.'

Even the toughest, brightest or most sociable young people go through the same rounds of unpleasant and sticky emotions. 'But how do I flip out of these thought spirals?' I can hear you ask. Read on.

None of us really realises just how powerful our thoughts are, but all you really need to know is this:

 Negative thoughts create misery and positive thoughts create harmony.

In this moment now, the thoughts you are having are creating your future. This means that **you have the power** to create the way you feel.

If you isolate one single thought and make it positive, it becomes like a laser beam. A concentrated focus of energy that can pierce through the fog of negativity that sometimes threatens to suffocate us.

Affirmations are a powerful way to change the way you feel.
Try it now. Put this book down and say, **'I can be whatever I want to be,'** over and over again in your head. How does it feel? Be honest.

If you feel weak and put upon by people, affirm:
'I am strong and powerful!'

and if you feel you may have failed in some way,
'I am a total success!'

It may sound crazy but it really works. Make up your own affirmation that works for you.

Make it fun for yourself. Repeat your affirmation as many times as you can throughout the day.

In the shower,
    eating ice cream,
        riding on the bus......
            roller blading.........
                putting your make-up on......

                    be creative!

You could even challenge yourself to repeat it 100, 200, 300 times a day.

Let the subconscious work for you at night

The most potent time to do affirmations is at night, just before you go to sleep.

Keep a diary and write down your affirmation ten or twenty times every night before you go to sleep.

If you make it the last thing you do before you go to sleep, then you will wake up feeling quite different!

While you are asleep the subconscious mind will process the information you have fed into it and empower it so that in the morning you will wake up feeling the effects. Try it and see!

Colours affect the way you feel

If you wear dark colours all the time - you may feel dark! Colour therapy is a whole science on its own and it has been proved that people are powerfully affected by the colours they wear and that surround them. Psychiatric patients, for instance, become agitated when the walls around them are red and calm down if they are pink or yellow.

Wear bright, vibrant colours and you will feel ... yes, you've got it - bright and vibrant!

Often teenagers wear black and grey because subconsciously they are trying to hide. Come out! Stop hiding! Wear red, yellow, white or turquoise blue. Get noticed and feel good about it!

Affirm: **I am attractive, and I'm special, just the way I am.**

Empowerment

In the Masai village near my home the initiation ceremony for five young teenage 'warriors' was taking place. I stood there, transfixed by the spectacle, as five thirteen-year-old young men stood tall and straight, their faces reflecting a story of self-power.

Their eyes were bright and their faces full of certainty and confidence. They were about to become adults - to be duly honoured and recognised by the elders of the community.

The whole village gathered around them in a circle, to welcome them into the adult world and the feeling of exultation and belonging was clearly marked on their faces.

- Mansukh

4 Empower yourself

Often, our modern Western society fails to adequately understand and cater for the powerful transition from childhood to adulthood. As a teenager, you can often find yourself alone, feeling separate and even disempowered. There may be a feeling of 'something missing' from your life and a desperate need to find an identity and sense of belonging. You may find yourself faced with challenges that you don't know how to deal with, such as:

1. **Relationship and sexuality problems** - that can create deep feelings of unworthiness and rejection.

2. **Low Self Esteem** - from not realising your power and greatness.

3. **Stress/Anxiety** - from exams and the pressure to achieve great things.

4. **Loneliness** - feeling isolated from your peer group, parents and family.

5. Aimlessness - having no real purpose or goal in life.

6. Feeling disempowered - by society and authority figures.

7. Depression - from feeling that life is not what you want it to be and not knowing how to change it.

8. Bereavement and loss - in relationships. Also parental divorce and the breakdown of the family unit may lead to insecurity and instability.

9. Drugs, Alcohol and Sex - the most powerful temptations around.

'No-one has ever taught me how to deal with all this stuff!'

It's true, isn't it? You can come out of school knowing all about maths, science and English - if you are lucky - but completely ignorant of how to relate to other people. You may know Kreb's Cycle inside out, but have no idea how to manage the stress and loneliness of being a teenager.

61

You may be afraid to ask for help, or not know where to go to get help with all the things you have to face in your life.

But all the answers - to every pain, question and confusion that you may have about yourself, your destiny and your life - are available.

Everyone wants to feel that life is exciting and fun, and drugs and alcohol may seem like an easy alternative to feeling bad, bored or just plain ordinary. They offer quick relief and a feeling of excitement, exhilaration and freedom - **but it's only temporary.**

They also offer long-term side effects that can destroy your life and the lives of the people who mean the most to you.

LSD can lead to a permanent personality disorder

ECSTASY (E) can lead to brain damage, strokes, depression and mental illness

ALCOHOL can cause blackouts, headaches, violence and fatal accidents

3 people die every 4 months from taking **E**

150 children die every year from **GLUE SNIFFING**

SPEED can produce paranoia and panic

SPEED can cause heart failure

SEXUAL PROMISCUITY exposes you to **HIV virus**, venereal disease and **unwanted pregnancy** and increases the risk of cervical cancer in later life

* ISDD, Drug Misuse in Britain 1996 - National Drugs Helpline - Alcohol Concern

63

'I'll only do it once, just to see what it's like ... I can handle it ... it will never happen to me.....'

We all have the freedom of choice, but the choices we make will determine what happens to us. This really hit me hard when I (Mansukh) was at university and four of my friends were killed in a car crash. It was so shocking to realise that drinking and driving can just wipe out your life. It probably seemed so innocent.....

We all know there is 'something more' to experience in life and it may be very hard to resist the pull towards 'quick kicks' and excitement.

Adam got involved in drugs because he was looking for excitement.

I was a misfit at school and doing drugs was different, alternative and exciting and made me feel good - for a while. I felt part of the sub-culture and thought straight people were weird because they couldn't see how much fun it was. I couldn't see anything wrong with it. I thought I had discovered the secret of life and how to be happy. I went to America and at a 'rave' accepted Ecstasy that had been 'cut' with Mescaline. Several days later I suddenly experienced a brief second of insight that what I was really looking for was a 'spiritual experience'.

A few days later I went into excruciating pain and knew that something was terribly wrong. I felt as though I was in a deep, dark tunnel, without any way out and I cried for hours on end. I knew I was in real trouble and overnight gave up drugs, alcohol and smoking.

Instead I took up swimming, yoga, chi kung and cycling. These have really helped me to get myself back together. I couldn't hang out with my friends in the drug scene any more and as soon as I accepted that, I started to meet people who understood real

65

spirituality without the dogma of religion. They really helped me to heal the damage I had done to myself. It's been a long haul, but I'm getting there.

Mark's experience of drugs was slightly different.

Between the ages of 16 and 26 my life revolved around getting money to get drugs, to change my state of mind and to escape from reality. I was searching for freedom, and drugs were the only way I could get this feeling. I actually became less free as my memory and will-power started to dissolve. I was looking for something meaningful, but experienced an ever-deepening feeling of emptiness.

My attitude was that as our modern medical practice is based on the use of drugs to relieve pain, why should society ask people not to try to relieve their emotional pain and bewilderment with drugs?

Then I met someone who started to teach me yoga and I learned how to change myself, to gain control of my thoughts and emotions. I realised that the feelings of contentment, peace and calm that I searched for through drugs were available to me for free and at any time, with no risk to my health.

As I learned to control the world inside me I found for the first time that I could control the world outside of me. Now I no longer need to escape from reality - because I can change it!

I started doing yoga and discovered an amazing interior world where I could control my thoughts and emotions and shape my experience of myself. It was under my control, not controlling me. It has given me more joy than any drug ever could.

Action plan - six steps to empowerment

1. Make a firm decision to **take responsibility** for yourself and have the courage to stand firm and be what *you* want to be - not what others want you to be. You have your own unique power and the techniques in this book will help you to access it.

2. Don't be afraid to **be original** - and don't let people pull you in a direction which you know is potentially dangerous to your health and disruptive to family and relationships.

3. **Make a firm commitment** to yourself to take the action that is necessary. Use the techniques in this book to help you to find purpose and meaning in life.

4. **Find safe, effective ways to feel good about yourself,** make a list of your good qualities and express them freely to others.

5. **Be open and willing** to accept all the help you need from others and find someone you can trust and talk to.

6. **Find positive things to do** that bring you fun and laughter. Really! It's better to be ACTIVE than bored and fed up!

 Do all these things in the right order!

5 Be fearless!

Young people are constantly doing things they have never done before.
First date, first party, first driving test ... just about everything is new,
isn't it? Sometimes you win and at other times you just can't seem to
match up to your hopes and expectations.

At these times you always have a choice. It's easy to go into a downward
spiral of negativity, feeling crushed, anxious and frustrated, or you can
approach things differently.

Successful people never accept failure, but use it as a stepping stone to
success. Does anyone ever do this? Yes! Anyone who is successful.
Behind many successful people lies a sea of failures.

 In fact, success arises out of well-made mistakes!

Eurowalk 2000 - teaching self-empowerment techniques at a Hertfordshire school, 1996

Did you know that **Christopher Columbus** was looking for India?

Walt Disney was fired from his job because he lacked ideas?

Albert Einstein's teacher described him as mentally slow? (He was expelled from school.)

The director's report after **Fred Astaire's** first screen test stated, 'Can't act. Can dance a little.'

Louis Pasteur came fifteenth out of twenty-two in chemistry.

Abraham Lincoln failed at everything he ever attempted to do and got only 200 votes in his first local election.

Every one of us has an unlimited potential, but we need to persevere and really believe in that potential no matter how many set-backs we have to face.

Bouncing Heels

Make your hands into fists and place them on the area of the kidneys. Fists point outwards.

Holding them firmly in place start to bounce up and down on your heels, keeping your toes on the floor.

Do this at least 18 times.

This movement removes fear.

Go for it!

1. For a few seconds imagine you are exhausted and depressed as on one of your worst days. Breathe slow, shallow breaths. Slump over and slouch! How do you feel?

2. Stand up straight as if you thought you were indestructible. Now breathe as though nothing could stop you in your life. Feel better?

3. Now stand strong as if you had just won the best race of your life and received first prize. Breathe deeply and powerfully. Feel your whole body, heart and mind on fire with enthusiasm and smile, so that your eyes sparkle.

Now in this extremely energised state, full of confidence and certainty - **try to feel sad.** You can't? Well, might as well stay happy then!

Clap Out of It!

If you feel sad, lazy or lethargic stand up straight and put your hands out to the sides with palms facing outwards.

Get ready to clap! Keeping the arms outstretched, draw the hands together in front of you and clap! In the same sweeping motion open the arms out again and repeat at least ten times.

Clapping stimulates energy and removes lethargy.

Yes, you can take the initiative

In 1991 the twelve year old daughter of a well-known environmentalist heard about the forthcoming Earth Summit in Brazil.

People from all over the world were invited to discuss the best way of preserving the environment, but no-one had asked any children to come and talk. Severn Suzuki made up her mind to do something about it.

Two years previously she had founded the Children's Organisation for the Environment. When she told her father that she felt that children should have a say in things, he suggested that if she could raise the money for the air fares, he would go with her to the Earth Summit.

Severn immediately took up the challenge. With the help of her friends she organised a funding drive with so much enthusiasm that the money simply poured in and six months later she was in Brazil.

Severn and her friends became celebrities at the Earth Summit, the only people invited to speak for the children of the world behind the closed doors of the governmental meetings.

As teenagers you need the freedom to explore life for yourself but at the same time you need to feel a firm foundation beneath you. Severn was lucky. She had the support of her father.

Amidst the turmoil of constantly-changing emotions and outbursts of self-expression you must be sure there is a stable rock to stand on where you are secure, loved and appreciated for who you are and who you are becoming.

Teenagers need encouragement! **This is where parents come in....**

The Crisis of the Parent/Teenage Relationship

Let's look at some common thoughts and feelings from teenagers:
- I love them but I wish they would leave me alone.
- They just don't understand me.
- They always stop me doing what I want.
- They are so stuffy and old fashioned and never listen to me.
- They treat me just like a kid.

and from parents:
- I can't seem to get through to them. They won't listen to me.
- Why do they have to dress in that way?
- I wish they would respect me more.
- I just don't understand why they have to behave like this.
- They never do what I want them to.
- They seem to want to hurt me.

How can I get on with my parents?

It's important to recognise that parents do have something teenagers lack, and that is maturity and experience. It's too easy to dismiss them as 'old-fashioned' or 'uncool' and just cut them off. Parents are wondering where their 'child' has gone.

For the parent

The transition from child to teenager seems very sudden and hard to adjust to. One minute they have a child on their hands and the next it's a rebellious, often aggressive and moody young adult who won't co-operate.

For the teenager

The transition is also dramatic. One day they wake up and simply don't want to be molly-coddled or 'pushed around' any more. Parents become irritating and something that hinders what 'they want to do'.

Co-operation and the miracle of love

Without co-operation parents and teenagers will never be able to see eye to eye.

The middle way

Parents have a tendency to try to mould their children into what they would like them to be. Teenagers want to explore for themselves what they would like to be and do not want to be moulded.

Teenagers have a strong sense of 'getting what I want' which can lead to behaviour that excludes parents completely.

any relationship between parents and teenagers a sense of love and co-operation from both parties is always the best way.

Raechel Waters, Antarctica 1996

My relationship with my daughter is a marvellous example of what I call the 'middle way'. She was young, active and full of life, wanting to move, expand and express herself in the world. I was cautious, protective and experienced.

There were many differences that came between us as she began to express her wish to do what she wanted. I was willing to grow, and willing to let her grow. So we began an experiment. I began to respect her for everything that she wanted but I would always be courageous enough to express my feelings honestly, without force or trying to impose my will upon her.

After a time we achieved what I now look upon as a very beautiful 'middle way'. We both learned so much about each other and we also learned how to co-operate. As a result she has grown up to be a confident, happy and stable human being and I have gained a great friend.

- Helena

Jump into each other's space

Make an effort to participate in each other's interests from time to time.

✓ You could take mum and dad mountain biking, roller-blading or share a vegetarian meal. Something that you love to do.

✓ You could go walking or swimming with them or whatever they love to do.

Close the generation gap - and create unity. It really works!

Parents - a child's eye view

4 years	*Mum and Dad are perfect - they can do everything.*
8	*They give me great presents.*
12	*They don't know much, do they?*
16	*Boy, they never lived and they definitely don't understand me.*
19	*They're so old-fashioned.*
23	*They know a bit. I suppose our holidays were quite good.*
29	*They gave up a lot for us, didn't they?*
32	*They really did their best.*
35	*I wonder if they'd like to see us more often?*
38	*I realise now that they really put up with a lot! They're very tolerant.*
45	*I wish I'd spent more time with them, because they did have a lot of wisdom!*
50	*If they were only here now, I would open my heart and say, 'I love you.'*

87

❖ Note for parents

If their foundation is based on loving support and filled with positive values that allow them to value themselves and their opinions, teenagers will become fulfilled and self-empowered as adults. If, however, it is based on a turmoil of aggression and empty values or immersed in constant arguments they will end up feeling very confused and rebellious.

Whether the teenage years are a spirited, pain-filled rebellion or a breath-taking exploration depends simply on whether the forces around them resist or encourage their growth. Either way you will grow. Few things are more certain than that **teenagers will find their own unique path in life.**

From the perspective of both parents and teenagers, you can make the most of the teens by recognising this great growth impulse and **getting behind it** rather than **resisting it.**

If you treat an individual...
as if he were what he ought to be
and could be, he will become what
he ought to be and could be.

- Goethe

Setting off in the Twenties

Decade of your dreams

*T*here's nothing quite like waking up in the twenties to that sunny morning feeling that says, 'It's so good to be alive! Yes! This is it! The world is my oyster and I am on the way to fulfilling my dreams!'

Perhaps you have finished your education, set off into an incredible relationship, picked up a job that will keep you going until your career really gets off the ground.....

Then of course, there is the rainy morning feeling when you wake up and panic. Self-doubt has set in. 'I'm on my own now! My whole future depends entirely on me and I'm not sure I have the strength to pull it off.' Setting off in the twenties can be thrilling and scary all at once as we start to realise all too clearly that no-one else is going to do it for us.

Have courage to explore

The twenties are a crucial time to begin to discover ourselves, our talents and **life itself.**

The crisis of the twenties can be one of not really knowing which way to go or which direction to take. Feelings of uncertainty and insecurity can easily persuade us to lean heavily towards the **'safe options'** in life and to follow the conventional slipstream.

It takes **real courage to follow your heart and dreams** because it will often take you in a direction that is unfamiliar and unknown.

If you find yourself wanting to go in a different direction from the safe 'norm' - **have the courage to do it.**

Making the Twenties an adventure

I (Mansukh) was lucky because my parents gave me permission and space to explore my life with a sense of adventure and anticipation. They instilled in me a sense that this was 'my time' and my opportunity. I always had a burning feeling in my heart that there was something I needed to find and I made sure that the search was on.

It is very fortunate to have the guidance of wise people as so many young people feel pressurised by their parents to follow a particular route that does not necessarily correspond with the call of their own heart. It's a bit like being on a train where society and conditioning are pulling us in a direction towards a safe, secure career. The twenties offer us our first opportunity to step onto the platform, to ask ourselves if we really want to go where the train is going.

 That step onto the platform is the bravest thing you will ever do.

93

David did it literally.....

I was sitting on the train, feeling very confused. Fresh out of university, my bags were packed and ready, and I was all set to go to London to meet my friends to look for work. Just before the train left the station an unexpected question came into my head. 'Why am I going there?' it said to me. 'Is it what I really want to do?'

It was an outrageous thought and one that I hadn't even entertained before. I was just following everyone else. The question shook me because I realised that I really didn't know why I was doing it. Suddenly something inside me said, 'Don't do it!' and without thinking I jumped up, got off the train and just stood on the platform watching it go. It felt scary but exciting to break away and stand on my own two feet.

 Have the courage and strength to listen to yourself.

Eurowalk 2000 - London to Birmingham

Confusion can be healthy!

What did David do next? He tried different things, all the time
exploring, seeking and searching for the 'right thing'. He travelled
around and came back feeling 'strangely contented'.

'I don't know what is wrong with David,' his mother told me. 'Can you
help him?' When I asked David what his problem was he said, 'I just feel
happy all the time! I don't know what I am going to do with my life, but
it feels OK! I'm a bit confused!'

I realised that he didn't have a problem and told him so!

Confusion is healthy - don't knock it! It can be a power-booster and the
beginning of an exciting new adventure. Like travelling through a
tunnel, all you have to do is to stay with it and wait for things to become
clear. They will!

- Mansukh

96

Choosing a career

It's a time when you may have to seriously consider a career and if so, choose something you feel really excited about. **What work is it you want to do? What are you good at? What do you enjoy the most?** You may know already and if you do, work towards your goal step by step.

Before choosing a career, it may be a good idea to take a year out to travel and explore things a little, because it will give you time to see your life from a distance. Travelling and experiencing different cultures expand our perspective and help us to learn acceptance of other attitudes and ways of living.

It's easier to see everything more clearly if you are away from the life and influences you have always known. Travelling gives us time to review and reflect on the journey we have made so far and the direction we want our life to take.

Do the things you really want to do

Marion couldn't think of anything she really wanted to do after finishing college and the last thing she wanted was to get caught up in a career path that didn't really suit her. When a friend suggested working on a farm that bred dogs, she jumped at the chance.

The work suited her down to the ground because she loved dogs and it was something a bit out of the ordinary. When her boss told her about the 2,000 mile Trans-Alaska dog-sled race, something hit home inside her. 'Now that really sounds like something I would like to do!' she thought.

She entered the race which turned out to be extremely gruelling but became the first woman ever to win it. In fact, she has gone on to win it three times. Life can surprise you if you give it the chance.

How can I make the most of my exploration?

1. Put your heart into it

Whatever you decide to do, whether it is travelling, university or exploring careers and relationships - **put your whole heart into it.** Really try to get as much from it as you can.

2. Keep a nice distance

Most importantly, **try to do it from a distance.** What does that mean? It means standing back and almost watching yourself doing whatever you are doing. Observe yourself as you move in and out of situations and encounters. **Become a witness** to events, as if you were watching a movie. You are involved, but you're *not* involved!

By doing this you will become more aware of yourself and get to know yourself more fully. This will set you up for making good decisions later in your life.

3. Get advice

Find out what you really feel about the things you are doing. How do they grab you? Is it really **you**? Talk to and be with strong, experienced people you respect and who know what life is about. Some of the most valuable people to talk to are those who have had the most failures in their lives and triumphed over them. Seek their advice and guidance.

Ask and you will receive
Seek and you will find
Knock and the door will be opened

4. Observe

Take a good look at those who are ahead of you in your chosen career. Talk to people who have done what you are thinking of doing and find out where it has taken them. Are they happy and fulfilled?

Each time my father took me out on to the Rift Valley plains at night, he would get me to prepare for it by doing these exercises for courage.

- Mansukh

The Sphinx   *'The Sphinx' is a preparation for 'The Snake' (opposite page)*

1. Lie down on your front with your forehead touching the floor, feet together. Place forearms and palms of your hands on the floor beside you, hands about eye level.

2. Breathe in and as you breathe out, lift your head and upper body so that you are now resting on your forearms. Breathe in.
On the out-breath slowly lower your body back down towards the ground.

102

The Snake

1. Lie down on your front, and clasp your
hands behind you.

2. On the out-breath lift your head and
upper part of the chest (focus on the
centre in your heart).... Power is
released by the neck movement and
strength is released by the chest
movement.

3. ..... keep focusing on the heart as you
lift your hands as high as possible. Hold
as long as comfortable, then gently relax
back into the starting position.

Affirm: May my strength and power
combine to give me full courage.

What if I don't give myself time to explore?

By the time we reach thirty we may find we will have to undo a lot of what we have already done. We can end up feeling that everything we've done so far has been wasted because we didn't take time at the start to question what everyone told us was the 'right thing' to do.

Inside every one of us lies a unique talent just waiting to express itself. It may be something that lights up the world or it may be something that silently opens the hearts of everyone around us. Either way, our happiness depends upon it. Do you have the courage to express that talent? Or is the fear of rejection going to hold you back possibly leaving you feeling unfulfilled at the end of your life?

**It doesn't matter what others think -
it's your life, go for it!**

Why settle for less?

I once heard someone say, 'But Mozart was a genius and I can never be like him. I'm just another Joe Bloggs.' I thought about that statement for days afterwards because it seemed to me that it represented a common dilemma: that of not being able to believe in one's unlimited potential.

The only difference between that person and Mozart was that Mozart had **identified** with his genius and believed in himself and his ability. He was simply not prepared to accept being plain old 'Joe Bloggs'.

- Helena

The famous Kenyan long distance track runner, Kip Keino, won the Olympic medal many times. No-one could beat him. When asked why he never boasted about his achievement, he said that it is because he knew that he wasn't the best. Over a hundred thousand of his countrymen could outrun him but - they didn't try.

Choose the right attitude

One of the most inspiring stories I have heard is about a little boy who was badly burned in a school fire. He was dragged unconscious from the flames dreadfully burned.

- Mansukh

Lying in his hospital bed he heard the doctor saying to his mother that he was sure to die, and that it would probably be the best thing considering that the lower part of his body was almost destroyed. But he didn't agree - and was determined to survive.

He did - and once he had pulled through the danger zone he again heard the doctor say to his mother that her son would be a cripple all his life. He didn't agree. He was determined to walk even though his thin, lifeless legs just dangled without any motor ability. Once home, while sitting in his wheelchair in the garden he threw himself onto the ground and started dragging his legs behind him.

Every single day, he dragged himself to the fence and hauled himself up on to his legs, pulling his little body along the fence. He was determined to walk and eventually he could stand up, then walk a little, then run.

He began running to school because he loved the exhilarating feeling of running and when he got to college he managed to get into the track team.

In his later years he ran the world's fastest mile. His name was Dr Glenn Cunningham.

Overcoming the fear of failure

Often the fear of failure holds us back from even **attempting** to use our talents. Try not to compare yourself with others to reinforce failure, but instead, be inspired to emulate the people you admire.

If you try and do not succeed, you will be in the same position as you were before you tried, except you will have learned something valuable. **If you never try, you may never learn.** Remember, success comes with just one step at a time.

> *There are no failures - only lessons and opportunities*
> *and every opportunity*
> *is another stepping-stone*
> *towards your goal.*

> *- Mansukh*

You can do it when you have to!

When I was twenty-two I delivered my first Outback baby in the isolated far north of Australia. She was born sixteen weeks premature and none of us expected her to live. It was four in the morning and I had only minutes to save her life. I feverishly recalled a recent posting in a high-tech maternity ward in Adelaide and made a humidi-crib from a cardboard box, plastic bag and kettle. I then set up a drip and massaged her sternum to keep her breathing.

It was touch and go but amidst all the pressure I felt so exhilarated to be saving a life in impossible conditions. I wasn't even qualified as a doctor yet, having two more years to do in college. You don't have to be up against it, but sometimes that is what it takes to prove to yourself you can do it.

- Helena

In the twenties you will need to build up and develop your physical, mental and emotional strength. This exercise works on all levels and is one that I have personally practised since I was a young boy in Kenya.

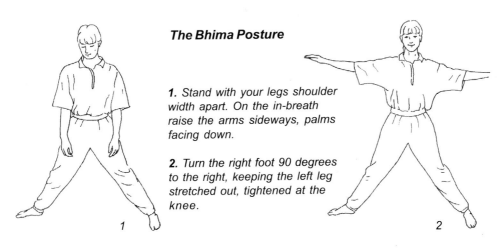

The Bhima Posture

1. Stand with your legs shoulder width apart. On the in-breath raise the arms sideways, palms facing down.

2. Turn the right foot 90 degrees to the right, keeping the left leg stretched out, tightened at the knee.

1

2

3. *Bend the right leg at the knee until the thigh is parallel to the floor.*
Place the right palm on the floor on the inside of the right leg and stretch the left arm up towards the sky. Look up at the left outstretched hand.

4. *Slowly stretch the left arm over your head to the right to form one line with the body. This stretches the whole of the left side of your body. Straighten up, taking care not to rush. Straightening the legs, come back into a standing position.*

Repeat on the other side.

3

4

111

Building Successful Relationships - (with almost anyone!)

The twenties are a time for opening up to **new people,** building relationships and learning intimacy. It's one of the most crucial aspects of this age. This does not mean just personal, loving relationships, but our association with **everyone** we meet.

The quality of our relationships with other people is dependent on the **quality of every interaction** we have with them. It means making a conscious effort to create positive feelings between each other, which takes awareness and skill in the art of communication.

In a nutshell, every human being responds to:

- Sincere care and concern
- Being listened to and understood
- Being respected for who they are

Get your relationships right in the twenties and you will be set up for life!

112

The law of resonance

I remember once asking my father why some people are not nice to be with. He went very quiet for a moment and then a half-smile flickered across his face.

Without a word he reached out for our two tanpuras (Indian stringed instrument) and placed them opposite each other. He plucked a string on one of them and immediately the same string began to vibrate on the other tanpura.

He looked at me. 'Start with yourself,' he said. 'What kind of resonance do you want to create in other people? Whatever strong emotion you are vibrating inside yourself will determine the echo response. Make sure you're in tune!'

– Mansukh

113

Creating resonance - giving people your best

In relating to others it's important to know that, like the tanpuras, we are always creating either resonance or discord. This means that if you approach someone with anger or irritation, you will immediately spark off an identical feeling in them. If you speak with love and gentleness, they will have no choice but to change and adjust to your vibration.

Whatever you put out will come back to you. This is a natural law.

In any relationship, whether with parents, boss, friends or lovers, how great would you feel if you always seemed to inspire their respect and love? Yes! It **is** possible! In love or work, the principles for creating great relationships are the same.

 The key is to avoid manipulating people with your hang-ups!

Outrageous strategy for creating resonance

✓ If you smile at everyone you meet, especially those at work, they will not be able to resist responding positively.

✓ Adopt an attitude of making the person/people in front of you happy. Do you know that it only takes twenty-eight muscles to smile and seventy-eight to frown? Be economical!

✓ If someone is aggressive or unpleasant use the **Invisible Heart Power Technique** instead of reacting (see page 120).

Try to remember that all anybody really wants is love, no matter how they are behaving.

An eye for an eye makes everyone blind

- Martin Luther King

Reach out of yourself to make others happy

In order to make a connection with someone we may have to adjust the way we act and be sensitive to them. For example if they talk quickly, it may not be a good idea to labour your words by speaking .... really .... slowly ..... it will drive them round the twist!

Try to step inside the person you are with and understand where they are coming from. What do they need to make them happy? A smile? A touch on the hand? A note of appreciation? A gift?

- Match the person's body language,
- their breathing pattern,
- then their conversation speed.
- Now guide them into a space that is important for the moment,
  e.g. if they are angry, be calm; if they are lazy, be really active.

Be bold in your communication

Imagine speaking your truth with honesty, positivity and an underlying care and concern for the person in front of you.

If you can learn just this skill it will enrich your life beyond recognition.

Everyone wants to be popular, valued, respected and loved by others. It's natural, but very often the reality is that our relationships are strained and difficult as people mirror our own fears and phobias.

If there is fear in our communication we find it difficult to build positive loving relationships. The biggest obstacle to being open to people and to exposing our own thoughts and feelings is often the fear of rejection. It takes courage.

Sometimes you have to take the first step.

Bill chooses heart power

We have known Bill for years. He is a wonderful character and the kind of person you feel happy to be with.

There's always one, isn't there? In every office you'll find one person that nobody likes or gets on with very well. You can't always put your finger on it, but there is something about them that just seems to get to you.

I had one of these in my office and one Monday morning I decided to approach him in a different way. Instead of ignoring him as I usually did, I turned to him and said, 'Would you like me to show you how to use my computer?' He looked disbelieving and didn't respond at all. I persevered and just kept asking, 'Do you want a bit of help with this?' It took a few days to win him round, but I did it.

It wasn't long before he became chatty and open, responsive and excited about learning this new skill, no longer sullen and withdrawn. I realised that the poor guy was just lonely and feeling rejected by everyone, which of course he was.

Bill's simple act of friendship transformed his friend's life.

119

Invisible heart power technique

♦ Take a deep breath and focus on the area of your sternum.

♦ Imagine a flow of energy coming out of your heart centre towards the person you find it difficult to get on with. You can either imagine they are there in front of you, or you can do it while you are talking to them.

Affirm silently but sincerely: I offer you good feelings and friendship.

Public Warning: This technique will seriously improve your life!

I once asked my mother how it was that everybody loved
her for she never seemed to have any conflict
with anyone at all.

'I taste my words before they leave my mouth, Manu,'
she said, 'to make sure that they don't hurt people.'

- Mansukh

121

Turning Thirty - the Great Opportunity

Thakor Patel - Life Foundation India

Turning Thirty - the Great Opportunity

Towards the end of the twenties we become increasingly aware that we have a potential waiting to be fulfilled, a kind of *whispering idea* that there is something of value to accomplish in life. For most of us this remains just an idea, a disquieting sense that the career or relationship we have worked so hard for is not quite bringing us the fulfilment we thought it would.

We might feel dissatisfied or frustrated and have thoughts like, 'I need more excitement,' or feel the need to change jobs, relationships, or to go on an adventure to recapture the thrill of our twenties.

Turning thirty brings us to a crossroads and a time to decide either to consolidate what we have already set up in our life or to change direction completely.

Deep questions start to come up inside us like, 'Have I realised my potential? Do I want to be doing this for the rest of my life? What is my purpose?'

It may be time to settle down and get married, or decide to have children and make a deeper commitment to a relationship or career.

Or it may be that life is calling us to make an interesting change.

The thirties are a challenge to step forward with courage and whatever we decide to do, put our **whole self** behind it.

Eurowalk 2000 - Ireland

I'm looking for excitement!

It always looks so inviting to pursue excitement in materialism - exotic holidays, fast cars, expensive houses, the latest hi-fi equipment and a wardrobe full of clothes. But the thrill of satisfying our every desire can leave us feeling even more disillusioned and frustrated because **it never lasts.**

We forget that it is not actually the fast cars that we want. It's the feeling we get when we are driving them that we are really looking for. It's not the relationship we are looking for but how the relationship **can make us feel.**

We can avoid being endlessly side-tracked by curbing material desires that just don't do it for us and **go for the real thing!** My ex-husband and I still laugh about the catalyst for my decision to go for it ....

It is not a Mercedes!

*In my thirties I was working as a psychiatrist and, like most people,
was completely immersed in the materialistic dream. My husband was
obsessed with the idea of a new Mercedes and one day he put his
dream into action and brought it home. I suddenly realised that this
car was not going to bring him the 'big happiness' he was looking for.*

*I could humour his dream, but once he had acted it out, it gave me
clarity about what was really important to me and I knew that I simply
had to get off the materialistic treadmill and search for something
more meaningful. I'd realised a Mercedes was not my sort of dream.*

- Helena

Something stirred in me as a result of that incident which meant that I had to take action to separate myself from that **illusion** of happiness. I wanted the real thing and my task was to find out what it was.

I started looking for it.

I found myself meeting people who had tremendous sense of purpose in their lives and were putting into practice what was still only a spark in my imagination. They had realised what was important to them and to humanity and were doing something about it.

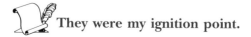 **They were my ignition point.**

Ignition point

A piece of wood doesn't look much until you ignite it. Then a miracle happens as the latent energy stored inside it becomes exposed and creates extraordinary heat, light and colour. We are all like this, packed with unignited potential just waiting for someone or something to set it alight.

Bob Geldof was just watching television when his passion to help the people of Ethiopia came alive. Within a month he had organised BandAid, the greatest act of global compassion in history.

It could be the sight of people living in cardboard boxes under Waterloo Bridge in freezing conditions that sparks you off, or meeting someone who is twenty years on in your chosen career and realising, 'Oh my God! Is that what I am going to be like!'

Some people wake up to an unknown depth of potential through tragedy which makes them reach out for greater strengths. Mairead Mcguire, a very special woman we met in Ireland on Eurowalk 2000, is a perfect example.....

Her life as a secretary suddenly became dramatically re-directed on 10th August 1976 when her sister, Anne, was walking along with her four children. An I.R.A. car suddenly hurtled round the corner chased by a British Army vehicle, lost control and careered onto the footpath killing three of her children. A young I.R.A. man was shot and Anne was left dangerously ill in hospital. It was a tragedy that brought Northern Ireland to its feet.

At the funeral, a tearful Mairead appealed to the people of Ireland in front of television cameras. 'This violence is wrong!' she cried out, and her pain was for every man, woman and child who had been killed in Northern Ireland.

Before long she had rallied thousands of women together and created The Peace People, who walked the streets together for peace in the most violent areas of Belfast. They brought mothers and children together across the divide and succeeded in pulling Northern Ireland back from the brink of civil war. Two years later she received the Nobel Peace Prize.

Mairead was forced to reach deep into herself and to listen to what her heart was telling her to do. She gave it everything she had and it has brought a powerful new meaning into her life and the lives of thousands of others.

It doesn't have to take a catastrophe to propel us towards our highest purpose, however. All it needs is the courage to follow a feeling....

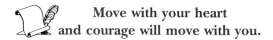

Move with your heart and courage will move with you.

Patanjali is the father of yoga and has been
one of the greatest inspirations of my life.

- Mansukh

*When you are inspired by some great purpose, some extraordinary
project, all your thoughts break their bonds.*

*Your mind transcends limitations, your mind expands in every direction
and you find yourself in a new, great and wonderful world.*

*Dormant forces, faculties and talents become alive
and you discover yourself to be a greater person by far
than you ever dreamed yourself to be.*

- Patanjali

*Your work is to discover your work
and then with all your heart to give yourself to it.*
                                                    - The Buddha

Finding your purpose

Imagine you are at a dinner party in your honour where everything has been laid on for you in the most beautiful way. Your family, friends and colleagues are all there. Three speakers are about to stand up to talk about you. They are going to tell everyone in the room,
who you are
what you have achieved and
how you did it.

What would you like them to say?

Stop here and write down exactly what you would like them to say about you, your life and your achievements. Without judgement or comparisons just let your highest aspirations for yourself flow out of you.

Congratulations! You have just described your own personal mission statement.

Whatever you have written down has the power to bring you real fulfilment. Imagine reading over what those three people have said about you and feeling, 'Yes! I've done it.'

Imagine the relief of feeling that you have accomplished what you came here for.

**You have discovered
what you really want to do with your life!**

Beware of the comfort zone

If you are feeling a sense of being trapped in a life you don't want and doing things you haven't chosen to do, you may have been in the comfort zone too long.

The comfort zone is the place where we feel safe and everything is familiar and known. It is a life scenario or set of circumstances we are accustomed to. At certain times in our life we feel the call to move out of it and into uncertainty. It can happen at any age!

It is a natural process and an evolutionary step. A deeper yearning is at work which contains both excitement and apprehension.

 Moving out of the comfort zone
will keep you very much alive and on the edge of your life.

Stepping out of the comfort zone

I don't think I ever made a conscious decision to step outside the comfort zone. All I knew was that what I was doing simply wasn't fulfilling me.

Becoming a consultant psychiatrist had been completely mapped out for me. The path was clear and I had so much support I could have reached the top of my profession, but something stopped me. It was too safe and predictable and I was bored because I could see my destination and everything in front of me for the next 35 years. I decided to leave the safety that would have led me to 'success'.

I had to cope with the constant rebukes of my peers who told me how irresponsible it was and what a waste of years of training. Didn't I realise I could have 'become this' and 'done that'?

I took a year out to do a postgraduate course. For the first time I found myself working in areas I didn't really know and had to learn to understand the concept of being five minutes ahead of other people. I felt challenged and stretched because it was quite scary and uncomfortable, but it was also very exciting and exhilarating!

Today I am so happy that I had the courage to make that decision. It has moved me into another depth of life.

- Helena

Make a momentous decision

Mohandas Gandhi followed a conventional career as a barrister, but this shy, timid man who was not particularly successful as a lawyer, made a decision overnight that was to affect not only the whole of his life, but the whole of India.

Late at night travelling through the South African Transvaal, he was thrown off the train for refusing to move into a third class compartment because of his colour. He sat shivering on the platform all night long, injustice and humiliation burning inside him. He had two options - either he could ignore the incident and carry on as before, or he could make a stand against the injustice of social prejudice. By morning he was sure that he had no option and his decision was the beginning of a new man and a new India. It was to lead him to become 'The Mahatma' or great soul.

M.K. Gandhi by Don MacKenzie

Later on Gandhi made the decision to free India and he then committed himself 100% to that goal. The power and depth of his commitment allowed him to go so deeply into himself that every ounce of energy he had available to him was dedicated towards that goal - and he **made it happen.** Commitment sets free the power of providence.

*If you go for your
highest purpose in life,
all the forces of the universe are with you.*

- Mansukh

139

The power of your commitment

It's impossible to find fulfilment in something you have only invested half of yourself into. If you are only half-committed to something, then you will only be able to put half your energy behind it and that, quite simply, is not exciting enough! Commitment gives us the **strength** to anchor our decision. It says, 'I will devote all my energy to this. Not half, not quarter - but all of it!' There is an old saying tells us:

> *If you give a little then a little comes to you.*
> *If you give more, then more comes to you.*
> *If you give everything - everything comes to you.*

Action plan - what can I commit myself to?

Sense which direction gives you the most inspiration although it may feel the most uncertain and the least safe.

Take out a piece of paper and write down:

✓ Three reasons you can do it.

✓ Why you really must do it.

✓ What attitude, ability and belief do you need to achieve it?

If you still don't find inspiration then ask yourself this. 'What will I miss out on in my life if I don't take this first step?'

Decide to make it happen and start now with one action, no matter how small.

141

Give yourself space to decide

◆   Be open to doing things that inspire you. Make time for things that make you feel life is good - being in nature, climbing, dancing, singing. Anything that makes you feel natural.

◆   Be prepared to take the blinkers off so you can see the clues that life is giving you as to what your next step might be and what is right for you to do. Remember that life is always leading you and never misleading you.

◆   Be with people who inspire and help you to believe you can achieve things you never dreamed possible.

The Gesture of Peace

The most important basis for making a good decision is a calm, clear mind. This sequence of gestures helps you to bring about a stillness in the mind that will enable you to make a clear decision.

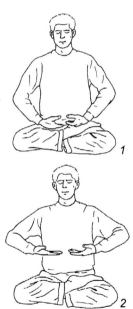

1. Sit comfortably on a chair or cross-legged on the floor with hands resting on knees, palms facing up. Become aware of the solidity of the ground beneath you. Hold in your mind the decision you need to make. Breathe in and draw your hands in towards your body. Hold and exhale.

Affirm: *All obstacles are now removed from my mind.*

2. Breathe in and draw your hands up to your solar plexus, and bring your fingers to face each other until your hands reach heart level. Pause and breathe out.

Affirm: *My heart is open. I welcome the future with excitement.*

3. *Breathe in and draw hands up to the level of face. Rotate the palms to face inwards. Breathe out and hold.*
Affirm: *My vision is clear. I know what I must do.*

4. *Breathe in and continue the movement upwards until arms are outstretched, palms uppermost, bent at the elbows. Lift the head slightly to look up. Pause naturally - exhale.*
Affirm: *I accept the power of my decision.*

5. *Now reverse the movement in the same four stages finally resting with palms on the knees, index finger and thumbs touching. Focus on the ground and feel the stillness and calm that follows.*
Affirm: *All my actions are now filled with conviction.*

145

Making that Difficult Choice

Are you one of the courageous few who are wanting to make a change in a new direction but don't know how? You may feel confused! Because so often everything else is pointing away from the direction you are bravely choosing to tread, you can feel out on a limb.

Sometimes it feels as if there is a lot at stake. Often a change in direction can mean that your circle of friends changes. You may have spent ten or fifteen years establishing a career or family. You may wonder what on earth you are doing and if it really is sensible and the right thing.

The answer is always YES! Trust yourself and your inner feelings.

 Go for what you really want in life and what is going to fulfil you.

It is the power of living on the edge of our own potential that will give us everything we are looking for.

- Mansukh

147

The Archer

Whether you decide to get married, to have that first child, to embark upon a new career, a world mission, or simply consolidate what you have, this movement will help you to point yourself in the right direction and go for it!

1. Stand with feet apart, back straight. Knees are soft, hands at heart level, palms facing each other, fingers relaxed. Turn left foot to the left, slightly bend right knee.

2. Raise arms to shoulder height at the same time extending the left arm out and up and bending your right arm at the elbow, as if beginning to draw a bow. The left hand holds the bow, right hand holds the string.

148

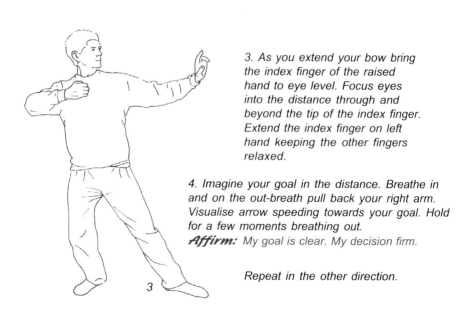

3. As you extend your bow bring the index finger of the raised hand to eye level. Focus eyes into the distance through and beyond the tip of the index finger. Extend the index finger on left hand keeping the other fingers relaxed.

4. Imagine your goal in the distance. Breathe in and on the out-breath pull back your right arm. Visualise arrow speeding towards your goal. Hold for a few moments breathing out.
Affirm: *My goal is clear. My decision firm.*

Repeat in the other direction.

149

Once a choice is made we are on our way

The thirties can be the most richly productive decade in our life if we give ourselves the opportunity to make it so.

We will need to put our heads down and get on with it because it is a time for hard work, a time for maturity and also a time to begin to understand the importance of commitment.

With the immense power of the thirties behind us we are building a life.

Our deepest fear is not that we are inadequate
- our deepest fear is that we are powerful beyond measure.
It is our light, not our darkness that frightens us.

We ask ourselves, 'who am I to be brilliant, gorgeous,
talented and fabulous?'
Actually, who are you not to be?

You are a Child of God.
Your playing small doesn't serve the world.

- Nelson Mandela

Building a Life -
A Formula for Success

Building a Life - A Formula for Success

Success lies in fulfilling your highest potential.

Success - means making the most of each moment and living at the very peak of your potential. If you are not empowering yourself and your potential you may feel bored or frustrated with an uneasy sense that something is 'not quite right'.

Happiness - is being able to rest in the place where you know that what you are doing and where you are going are **just right for you**.

Great things are done by people who think great thoughts and then go out into the world to make their dreams come true.

- Ernest Holmes

At one of our Eurowalk seminars recently we met Damian who told us that the only thing he had ever wanted to do was to become a doctor. When he didn't get the 'A' level grades, he felt crushed and devastated.

I drifted into the first thing that came along - accountancy - but could never escape the feeling that it wasn't what I really wanted to do with my life. I was successful enough, but as I entered my thirties I became more and more dissatisfied. Mr Nice Guy on the outside, I was a seething mass of resentment on the inside. The only relief I had was Friday night at the pub where I could drink to forget how much I hated my life.

I got involved in a relationship with another woman which led to a messy divorce and from then on things just went from bad to worse. My health began to deteriorate but the doctors couldn't help me. In desperation I tried homoeopathy.

*To my amazement it worked! I could hardly believe that something so simple could have such a dramatic effect and I became instantly fascinated by the process. I started a part-time course at a homoeopathy college which turned out to be **the best thing I've ever done**.*

I had never met such friendly people in all my years in the business world and I began to discover that I could use homoeopathy to help people, which is what I had always wanted to do. At last I had found direction in life and a way to achieve my dreams!

It took me quite a few years to develop a practice and make the change away from accountancy but it has been worth it. I have learned to be kind to myself which I hope makes me kinder to others and now I look forward to every day and wake up feeling happy and excited. I cannot think of a single area in my life which hasn't dramatically improved now that I am doing what I really want to do.

A Five Point Strategy for Success

In order to achieve our highest potential **at any stage of life**, we need a strategy - and this is it!

1 *Set your goal*

Imagine trying to fire an arrow without having a target. Pointless? A life without a goal means that your life just drifts along guided by chance or 'luck'. All your energy will be simply wasted because **if you do not know where you are going, you will never get there.**

Goals give us clarity, momentum and direction in life. It sounds simple enough, but most people find it very difficult to recognise what they really want from life.

Give yourself time to decide what you want. Make your goals **realistic**, **challenging** and **worthwhile** and give their achievement **high priority.**

Be determined to make the effort to realise them.

Whatever you think about the most is what you will gravitate towards, so if you fix your mind on your goal, you will naturally tend to move towards it.

Aim high because the smaller your goal the less inspiration you will feel. If your goal is to get french fries - that is all you will get!

> *The higher your goal, the higher*
> *the inspiration you will feel.*
>
> *- Mansukh*

We recently heard about John Goddard who is a great example of someone who has really grasped the concept of goal setting!

He made a list of 127 goals he wanted to achieve in his life. To date, he has achieved 108 of these goals which include climbing 12 of the highest mountains in the world, swimming in 5 of the biggest lakes, studying primitive cultures in 12 countries, circumnavigating the globe 4 times and milking a poisonous snake (which bit him) to name but a few!

He set his goals at the age of fifteen and continues to make it his life's purpose to achieve them all. Among his remaining goals he has yet to read the entire Encyclopaedia Britannica, climb Mount Everest and live to see the 21st century (he'll be seventy-five).

Action plan - goal setting

✓ **Make lists**. Spend five minutes writing down your goals every day.

✓ **Write down three ways** to take immediate action towards achieving those goals.

✓ **Set a time limit** e.g. I will achieve this goal in five days.

✓ **Focus all your energy** on these actions.

✓ **Review your main goal** every day and general goals every week.

This sequence of hand gestures is an ancient temple technique which enhances our ability to get excited about our personal goals and to tap into deep resources of energy within us. It is the most successful method that we have yet found for anchoring the energy to achieve your goal.

- A sequence of movement, breath and inner visualisation, it creates a link between all the energy centres in the body and our chosen goal.

- It will turn your goal into something that will benefit everyone.

- It will enable you to follow your goal with a calm, focused mind as opposed to an agitated, scattered one.

The only two criteria for this technique are that you must be **sincere** and **consistent**.

Gesture of Goal Setting

1. Sitting comfortably with a straight spine, raise your arms out to the sides at shoulder height with palms facing forwards.

2. Breathe in, and as you breathe out, bend the right elbow and draw the arm towards you, fingers facing forward and up.

3. Place your left hand, palm uppermost, underneath the elbow of your right arm. With the palm of your right hand facing forward, imagine your goal is there in front of your hand.

4. Encircle your goal with a royal blue light.

1

3-4

161

5. Now draw the fingers around the blue light, closing the fist - firmly capturing your goal, at the same time turning your fist to face towards you.

5

Affirm: **My goal is now firmly anchored. Success is inevitable.**

2 *Believe it is possible*

Your ability to act decisively with energy and enjoyment depends entirely on your faith in yourself. **Do you really believe you can do it?**

Imagine how your life would be if you were using all your potential and energy. Nothing could stop you! In contrast, thinking about failure completely sabotages any *chance* of success. Always say, **'It is possible,'** no matter how 'impossible' it may appear to be. If you have conceived it in your mind, then it is possible and if you can imagine it - and see it in your mind - **you can do it.**

Contemplate the word IMPOSSIBLE and break it down like this:

I M POSSIBLE!

The power of belief will help you achieve the impossible.
*One day a student happened to be sleeping while his professor wrote
a mathematical problem on the blackboard. The student thought it
was the week's homework - and handed it in a few days later, solved,
remarking how difficult it was.*

*The professor was amazed. He'd written it up because the problem
had never been solved before! By thinking the problem had been
given as homework, the student believed he ought to be able to solve
it - and so he did.*

The beliefs we have about ourselves and our life are what will determine
the outcome of our actions. We have only borrowed them from others
according to the messages we have received. Their foundation is based
on the fact that criticism meant pain to us and praise equalled joy.

Whether you believe you can or you can't, you are right!

- Henry Ford

Someone only has to say, 'You don't look well,' and you can spend the whole day thinking you have cancer! Or if they say, 'You cannot do it,' and you **believe** them, it can affect your whole experience of life. Here's another example of belief in action.....

The headmaster of a large secondary school in California recently invited five teachers into his office. 'Congratulations!' he exclaimed. 'You have been chosen because you have the greatest potential in our school. We would like to give each of you a class for a year, specially made up of talented students with the greatest all-round ability.' The results were astonishing. After a year these five classes achieved the highest results in the whole state. In the end the headmaster disclosed the real experiment. 'Actually,' he smiled, 'you have done far better than you realise. You see, the selection process wasn't based on potential. You and your students were all picked at random, but by believing you were the best, you became the best!'

Action plan

Test the power of positive belief

1. Stand with your feet apart, raise both your hands to shoulder height and twist around to one side. Go as far as you can without straining and then come back to the front.

2. Now, close your eyes, and without raising your arms, imagine doing the same thing - and turning around 360 degrees.

3. Now open your eyes and do the movement again. See how you can turn much further!

Well done! You have just replaced an outmoded 'underbelief' about yourself. You haven't just become more flexible because that's not possible in one movement. You have just created a new and greater belief in your ability. And this is just the start ... Let's go!

3 *Use your energy effectively*

Successful people know exactly where they want to go and pull in all their resources and energy to channel in the direction of their goal. People without clear goals just drift from one thing to another, frittering and wasting their energy, with a nothing result.

Once you have your goal in sight you will need to put all your emotional as well as physical energy behind it. See the Golden Triangle on page 180.

Successful people have a clear discrimination between what they choose to get involved in and what they don't. Recognise where you waste time in activities that don't take you towards your highest goal and where you really want to go.

 Spend most of your time in the area of your goal.

Successful people prioritise

Learn to prioritise what is important and essential. If, for instance, the most important thing in your life is having a happy family life and you spend 90% of your time at work, you will only be successful in that area if you cut down your working hours.

You may need to

✓ Be very discriminative about how you socialise.

✓ Switch off the TV three or four times a week.

✓ Avoid mindless entertainment that doesn't take you towards your goal. (Unless of course your goal is to waste time and resources!)

 Failure does not exist - only opportunity.

Keep your energy happy

✓ **Keep yourself energised** by making healthy, vital food and exercise part of your normal day. (Make sure you lead the dog, and not the other way round!)

✓ **Please do not bring your work home** - just yourself! On your way home from work, stop the car near a park and walk or stretch for ten minutes so you can return rejuvenated and alive again after clearing away the stress of a day at work.

✓ **Use relaxation and energy-balancing exercises** like the ones in **The Golden Triangle** programme (see page 203) to clear away energy blocks and accumulated toxins.

Some of the most successful people
have achieved their goals through these methods.
Become one of them!

4 *Take responsibility for your life*

Responsibility is the **ability to respond**. It is about learning to act wisely and in such a mature way that in all circumstances your actions uphold and support the lives of others. People who take responsibility take on the commitment to care for others by learning to be in charge of their own lives and emotions.

Those who have understood true responsibility have real freedom because they are able **to act** and **not react** in any given situation.

You will never find a successful person blaming the world if things don't work out. They know and believe that their life is not just a haphazard arrangement, and that **you are in charge of your life** and no-one else.

In order to achieve our goal, **we must take full responsibility** for everything that happens to us. 'Failure' is seen as a learning experience and part of the whole process of achieving success.

Thomas Edison failed 9,999 times to create a light bulb. Someone once asked him if he could bear to fail a 10,000th time and he looked at them in total disbelief. '10,000 failures?' he exclaimed. 'All I've done is learn 9,999 ways of how not to create the perfect light bulb!' In fact, **he did succeed on the 10,000th attempt** and he had used his 'failures' to get there.

An attitude of taking responsibility means you will think things like, 'Right! I'm going to use this setback to get further towards my goal.' If you carry on this process again and again you cannot fail because **failure** then becomes a very relevant part of your life.

 Failure is only something in your mind that gives you permission to give up.

Consider this:

Abraham Lincoln failed at just about everything he set out to do. In fact, his life was a veritable catalogue of disasters.

At the age of ...		
	31	- his business failed
	32	- defeated in a legislation race
	34	- his business failed again
	35	- his fiancee died
	36	- had a nervous breakdown
	38	- lost a local election
43, 46 & 48		- lost a congressional race
	55	- lost a Senatorial race
	60	**- became the greatest President of the USA**

Failure? I never encountered it. All I ever met were temporary setbacks!

- Dottie Walters

Action plan - self responsibility

Before we can take responsibility we need to have compassion for ourselves.

Use the Peace Gesture in 'The Thirties' page 144 but substitute **these** affirmations at each point.

Position 1.   *I take total control of my energy.*

Position 2.   *I open myself to compassion and understanding.*

Position 3.   *I take full responsibility for my own will.*

Position 4.   *I am in total control of my life.*

5 *Communicate your potential*

What you communicate is what you are

Once you are fully committed to your decision and believe you can achieve it, effective communication becomes essential.

This is the most important skill you will ever need because **unless you can communicate** whatever you have learned **your life cannot take off in the way it should.**

Successful communication depends to a large degree on the words we choose to use. Try to be precise in your statements and not to make sweeping generalisations and assumptions or use vague, unspecific language.

✓ **Be clear and specific:** You will have already noticed that people whose conversation is vague and generalised create a' fuzzy' kind of feeling around them. You can't quite make out what they want or how to deal with them. It is very important to communicate clearly your needs and wishes.

✓ **Question yourself:** If you hear yourself saying something like, 'I can never get on with farmers,' just ask yourself - 'Never?'

Of course it isn't true, because you haven't met them all. If you were to be *specific* you would say, 'I haven't been able to get on with the farmers I have met so far.' This cuts out all the vague areas.

✓ **Take one situation at a time** on its own merit and act on it with a clear perspective of what you want to achieve in that moment.

Internal Dialogue

The way we talk to ourselves internally determines the quality of our communication. If our own inner language is precise and specific, positive and empowering, that is how we will communicate verbally to the world. Quite often we will talk to ourselves in a way that is negative without realising it. Our inner dialogue may follow this kind of route:

'Why is that guy cutting me up?'
'Doesn't he know how insensitive that remark is?'
'Oh God! Why do the lights have to go red now?'

This kind of inner questioning doesn't bring positive results! It just winds you up and makes you turn red, feeling insensitive and cut up! If you find yourself saying, 'I could never do that,' question yourself immediately. What would happen if you could?

 Talk to yourself positively!

Have solutions ready

It's vital to create new, positive internal thought spirals. This means addressing ourselves in the right way and adopting attitudes that are helpful and constructive.

For example, we might say, 'Ok! This has happened. Never mind, let's just pause for a moment and take stock.'

Or, 'The lights are red so I have a few moments to think about what I need to do today and who I need to contact.'

Our dream happens moment by moment, in every interaction. We have to prepare ourselves internally **all the time** in order to be in the 'right space' so that when we meet each moment, we are ready for it.

> *Life is a series of moments -*
> *each one is at our disposal waiting to be exploded.*
>
> *- Anon*

Action plan - pro-active energisation

We can simply react to the events of each moment, doing lots of things but getting nowhere.
Or we can be **pro-active**. This means we take the energy we've tapped into and **use it** in a conscious and deliberate way to make that moment work for us.

It is possible to communicate our highest potential all the time.

Exercise - Record yourself talking on a tape recorder. Listen back. Are you impressed? Do it again and again until you are!

 Our interactions can be passive or active. Be active!

Energised action is the making of our dreams.
- *Mansukh*

Thakor Patel - Life Foundation India

The Golden Triangle

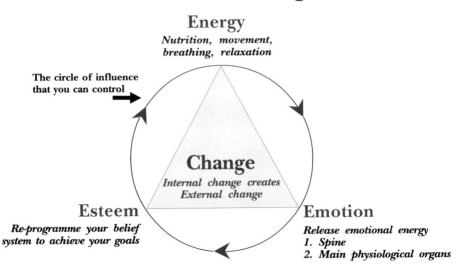

Energy
Nutrition, movement, breathing, relaxation

The circle of influence that you can control

Change
Internal change creates External change

Esteem
Re-programme your belief system to achieve your goals

Emotion
Release emotional energy
1. Spine
2. Main physiological organs

The Golden Triangle Programme

Any attempt to be successful in life, no matter what situation you find yourself in, will require one element above everything else. Energy! Without it you cannot do anything at all.

The **Golden Triangle Programme** will help you to access your deepest resources of both emotional and physical energy.

An abundance of this combined energy will allow you to experience a tremendous sense of well-being and dynamism. You'll feel just fantastic!

All it takes to raise your energy to 70-80% efficiency so that you can constantly engage in a powerful pro-active state is - twenty minutes of your time every day.

The three principles of the Golden Triangle - the three E's:

Energy
Physical energy and vitality - a powerful physical force.

Emotion
Emotional energy - a powerful creative force.

Esteem
Thought is energy - positive thought gives us the power to control and direct all our energy towards our goals.

1 Energy

Take care of your body and your body will take care of you.

In order to optimise our energy, first of all we need to learn to access our physical energy effectively.

We need to take into consideration these four factors:
 a) - Diet and nutrition
 b) - Physical movement
 c) - Breathing
 d) - Relaxation

The health of the people is really the foundation upon which all their happiness and all their powers as a state depend.

- Benjamin Disraeli

a) - **Diet and Nutrition**

- Do you wake up feeling tired and exhausted?

- Did you know that eating after 8pm could be a major cause of your lack of energy? Instead of your body's energy being available for rejuvenation during sleep, it becomes diverted towards the digestive process which takes up to eight hours to complete.

  If you look at when, what and how you eat, you can increase your energy by 60 - 80% within a fortnight!

  Follow the golden vitality tips on page 186.

Diet and Nutrition Course, Snowdon Lodge, North Wales.

Golden Vitality tips

✓ Eat more grains, pulses, vegetables and fruit and less oil-based and animal foods.

✓ Eat fresh wholesome foods wherever possible - salads, greens and sprouted foods.

✓ Avoid processed, lifeless foods such as 'microwave dinners'.

✓ Avoid heavily refined foods like sugar and those with a lot of synthetic additives like canned drinks and biscuits.

✓ Overeat only once a week!

✓ Minimize your intake of stimulants such as alcohol, cigarettes and red chillies!

✓ Eat in a calm environment with a relaxed attitude.

✓ Chew your food well as a lot of energy is absorbed in the mouth - take it easy, eating's not a race!

✓ Combine your foods skilfully. (See chart over)

✓ Eat only when hungry.

✓ Try to prepare and cook your food with care and attention.

✓ Finish your last meal of the day at least four hours before sleeping.

Major golden tip - enjoy it!

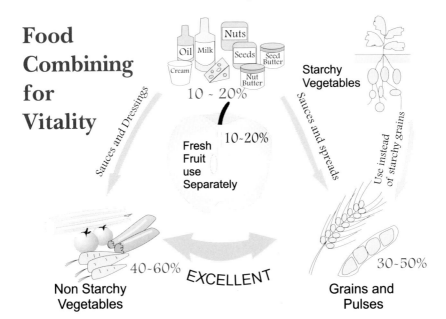

Food Combining for Vitality

Sauces and Dressings

Nuts
Oil
Milk
Cream
Seeds
Seed Butter
Nut Butter

10 ~ 20%

Starchy Vegetables

Sauces and spreads

10-20%
Fresh Fruit use Separately

Use instead of starchy grains

40-60% EXCELLENT

Non Starchy Vegetables

30-50%

Grains and Pulses

The Golden Triangle Programme

Food Combining for Vitality

Cold Pressed Oils
olive, sesame, sunflower, soya

Dairy Products
butter, cream, milk, cheese, yogurt

Others
margarine, avocados, olives, coconut, nuts, seeds, nut butters

Starchy vegetables
potatoes, pumpkins, parsnips, sweetcorn

Fruit
bananas, grapes, melons, blackberries, grapefruit, oranges, pineapple, raspberries, strawberries, apples, pears, apricots, cherries, kiwis, peaches, dates

Non-starchy vegetables
broccoli, spinach, cabbage, sprouts, cauliflower, courgettes, celery, kale, aubergines, peppers, carrots, swedes

Grains
rice, millet, barley, wheat, rye, oats, bread, pasta

Pulses
chickpeas, split peas, lentils, Beans: aduki, soya, mung

189

b) - Physical Movement

The law of physics states that the passing of fluids through magnetic fields produces electromotive power. Aerobic exercise sets in motion the flow of liquids such as blood and lymph through the magnetic fields of your body, producing an abundance of internal magnetic energy.

Movement is the second crucial factor in accessing our deepest levels of physical energy. The following programme will tone and energise your whole system if practised regularly and with commitment.

Eurowalk sponsor – Sally Line

The Sun Sequence is thousands of years old. The Ancients have always recognised the sun as a major source of energy and vitality and this sequence taps into the solar centre of energy within us.

Do it every morning and it will set you up for the day. If you can face the rising sun even better! Start today and be amazed!

The Sun Sequence

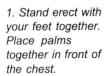

3. *Bend forward until the fingers or hands touch the ground outside the feet. Keep legs as straight as possible.*

4. *Taking your weight on your hands, stretch the right leg back as far as possible. At the same time bend the left leg, but keep the calf at right angles to the floor. Both hands rest on the left knee.*

1. *Stand erect with your feet together. Place palms together in front of the chest.*

2. *Raise both arms in front of you and above your head. Keep the arms separated by a shoulder's width. Bend the head and upper body slightly back.*

The Sun Sequence

6

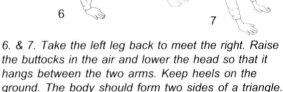

7

5

5. Place both hands either side of the left foot.

6. & 7. Take the left leg back to meet the right. Raise the buttocks in the air and lower the head so that it hangs between the two arms. Keep heels on the ground. The body should form two sides of a triangle. Keep legs and arms straight in the final position.

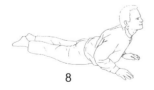

8

8. Lower the body to the ground and then raise the head and chest, keeping the navel on the ground and arms bent.

193

The Sun Sequence continued.....

9

9. *Lower the body onto the floor and come into a press-up position. Bring the right leg forward so that the calf is at right angles to the ground and the left leg stretches back as far as possible. Place both hands on top of the right knee, left over right.*

10

11

10. & 11. *Place your hands alongside your right foot. Take your weight onto your hands and bring the left leg forwards to meet the right. Raise into a forward bend. Uncurl slowly back into the standing position.*

If you find you are short on time you could just perform certain parts of the Sun Sequence on a daily basis.

Suggested programme

Monday   - Positions 1, 2 and 3
Tuesday   - Positions 4 and 5
Wednesday - Positions 6, 7 and 8
Thursday   - Positions 9, 10 and 11
Friday   - Positions 2, 3 and 4
Saturday   - Positions 6, 7 and 8
Sunday   - Positions 1 and 2

If you start walking you find yourself sleeping better, enjoying your extra energy flow, digesting your food comfortably, having a trim lean body, increased awareness and prone to attacks of cheerfulness and optimism.

*- William Finley and
Marion Weinstein*

Margaret McCreery and Jean Weldon

Walking

Walking is one of the most obvious and beneficial forms of physical movement. It is also one of the most powerful tools to access physical energy. Our experiences with Eurowalk 2000 have shown us that walking at a fast, but enjoyable, pace with intention and awareness is one of the best ways to purify the body and mind.

As we walk, energy comes naturally and we find ourselves feeling alive and energised, full of creativity, new ideas and enthusiasm. Once we free up our innate life force, energy begins to flow spontaneously and effortlessly. Try it and see.

For any problem that you have in life, regardless of the magnitude, try 10 -15 minutes brisk walking a day and feel its magical effect.

 Never underestimate the power of walking!

c) - Breathing

Apart from food, breath is our greatest source of physical energy. Through conscious use of the breath we can awaken and energise the body in seconds.

Proper breathing requires the use of the diaphragm. When we breathe fully, the diaphragm contracts and the abdomen expands, allowing the lungs to fill with air. Most people use only a fraction of their lung capacity which means that energy and vitality will be extremely diminished.

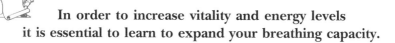

In order to increase vitality and energy levels it is essential to learn to expand your breathing capacity.

Action plan

The Full Breath

Sitting as straight as you can, inhale by expanding first the abdomen and then the chest in one, slow movement until the lungs feel full of air.

Exhale by relaxing first the abdomen and then slowly push the breath out with the diaphragm, as the chest relaxes.
Create a natural pause at the end of the inhalation and the exhalation.

For an alternative energising breath, please refer to page 236.

d) - **Relaxation**

Relaxation is an integral part of health. We need to relax in order to allow the body to adjust and recharge.

When you activate the body's relaxation response the brain secretes natural relaxants which soothe away the stresses of a busy day. You may only need fifteen minutes to completely revitalise yourself.

Used in combination with movement and vigorous exercise, relaxation will maximise the energy available to you. So if you want to feel brighter and happier, put on some soothing music and settle into a deep and rejuvenating relaxation like the one opposite.

Waves of Peace Relaxation Exercise

- To activate the relaxation response, lie flat on your back, legs and arms spread out a little, palms facing uppermost.

- Become aware of your breath for a few minutes.

- As you breathe in, rotate your feet outwards, letting them come back as you breathe out. Simultaneously allow your arms and hands to rotate outwards and then gently rotate back towards the body.

- After a few minutes gradually let your feet and arms come to rest. Continue in blissful relaxation for as long as you need to.

2 *Emotion*

The emotional energy that we have within us is an extremely creative force. It either flows freely throughout our body or is stored in little pockets as blockages that hinder our lives. Most of us are unaware of this vast potential. The truth is that we can either use it for empowering ourselves and our goals, or we can allow it to drain us completely. Tap into this energy source and you will be amazed at just how much energy will be made available to you!

The two main areas that hold emotional energy are
a) - The spine and
b) - The main physical organs, particularly the liver, lungs and kidneys.

The following two exercises will allow you to set this energy free.

a) - Spinal Release

1. Standing upright and straight, spend a few moments focusing on your breath with eyes closed.

2. Breathe in, and on the out-breath allow the head to bend forward. Breathe in again and as you breathe out, let the spine bend forward a little bit more.

3. Continue in this way with each breath, slowly allowing the spine to bend down one vertebra at a time, keeping the chin tucked into the chest until you reach a natural limit.

4. To come up reverse the movements. Remember that all movements happen on the out-breath, with pauses on the in-breath. The head comes up last.

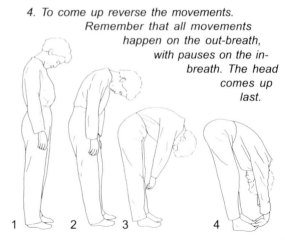

1   2   3   4

b) - The CNS (Central Nervous System) Breath

Stimulates the main organs in the body

1. Stand with feet apart and knees soft. Place your left hand at the level of the navel, palm facing upwards. Place your right hand above it, palm facing down.

2. Breathe in and start to raise your right hand up to the level of your eyes. Breathe out.

3. Breathe in and turn the palm to face upwards and raise your hand up about a foot above your head. Breathe out.

4. Breathe in and as you breathe out start to lower your arm to the side as far as shoulder level. Breathe out.

5. Without moving your body, let your arm move out to the side as if someone is pulling it. Rest.

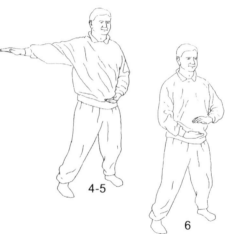

4-5

6

6. Breathe in and on the out-breath bring your hand to the navel position with palm facing upward and left hand above it, facing down. Repeat the movement on the other side.

This sequence can also be used as an adjunct to 'The Salutation to the Four Directions' (please see Dr Patel's book 'The Dance between Joy and Pain')

3 Esteem

Within each one of us there is a belief system that determines how our lives will be. If we want to change any aspect of this system of belief we will need to .....

a) - Release old patterns that inhibit us

&

b) - Reprogramme ourselves for success.

Releasing Old Patterns

1. Stand with legs about three feet apart, knees bent, feet slightly splayed.

2. Lean forward and place your hands on the thighs above the knees.

3. Supporting yourself with your hands breathe in and push the base of the spine backwards, elongating the spine, curling the upper back up and raising the head.

4. Breathing out tuck the tail under, arch the upper back up and lower the head.

All movement begins at the base of the spine.

The Standing and Twisting Cat
- perform together

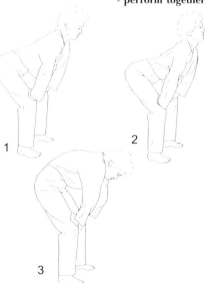

207

The Twisting Cat

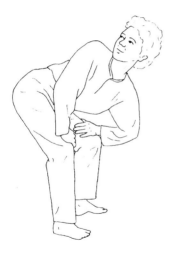

1. From the Standing Cat bend the knees a bit more.

2. Breathing out lower the right shoulder down turning the body to the left.

3. Relax, breathe in and straighten up.

4. Breathing out, lower the left shoulder down in the same way, turning the body to the right.

For re-programming the mind and body for success

1. Stand up straight and place your right hand under the left. Join tips of the thumbs together. Quietly and affirm to yourself, I am strong and powerful.

2. Gently move your hands together in front of the sternum and affirm: I have the energy to succeed.

3. Push your hands upwards towards the sky. As your hands separate and come down either side of you, begin to affirm: I am willing to learn and grow from my mistakes.

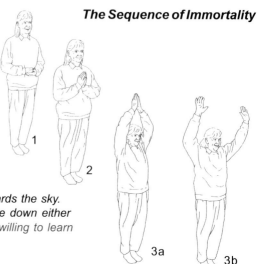

The Sequence of Immortality

4. Right fingers point upwards and left down towards the ground and affirm: *I have the courage to face all challenges.*

6. Hands return to **second** position and affirm: *I am a total success.*

5. Join thumb and forefingers in this position and affirm: *All my actions benefit everyone.*

What will determine the quality of the benefits that you will experience by using the Golden Triangle programme?

These 3 magical rules.

1. Sincere regular practice
2. ..... a little bit more
3. ..... and a little bit more than that!

Remember to have fun and really enjoy yourself!

Obstacles are those frightful things you see

when you take your eyes off your goal.

- Henry Ford

Overcoming the Obstacles to Success

Conditioned belief patterns run deep! One client expressed it this way:

I got really excited when I realised that yes! I can have what I want! I don't have to settle for second best any more! I decided what it was that I really wanted to achieve and it felt so good.

Then 'circumstances' conspired against me and everything moved towards second best again. I felt resigned but bitterly disappointed. Everything inside me was saying, See - you can't have what you want. I even detected a little voice saying, You don't deserve it anyway.

What do I do now?

It is important to understand that the signals from our conditioned belief patterns come up on automatic from the sub-conscious mind. These self-limiting beliefs are not reasonable.

It takes time, patience and **applied skill** to believe in your ability to succeed, so try not to set yourself up for failure.

> **Make it easy to reach your goal
> and impossible to miss.**

Small success leads to big success

People think they have to achieve great heights to feel successful, and that the higher the goal, the greater the feeling of success. But the feeling you get from a small success like someone telling you that you are wonderful, can be the same as winning a million pounds.

> As a boy I would walk around with a catapult in my pocket that my Dad had made for me. I went out into the fields every day and lined up a row of tin cans. I always picked a distance that ensured I would never miss. Gradually I increased the distance, but never more than I could master. This programmed success into my psyche.
>
> *- Mansukh*

Action plan - build a success habit

✓ Work at something very simple and effective every day that gives you a feeling of **achievement** and **confidence.** It must be something you know you can do well. It could be as simple as throwing a tennis ball against the wall twenty times a day. What are you waiting for? Go and get a ball!

✓ It could be something as silly as getting up in the morning and making toast *(with* marmalade) or playing darts with your friends.

✓ **Make a list** of three things you know you can do. Choose the one you *really feel excited about* - **and do it now!**

✓ **Practise** it every day. See yourself succeeding every time you do it. This is the way to build your success habit effectively.

 Remember that a habit means again and again and again and again.....

217

Making success out of failure

Stage 1. Become aware - awareness can create space in your mind for possibilities other than the one you are seeing or experiencing.

Stage 2. Ask the right question - using awareness, ask yourself, 'Can this situation actually benefit me?'

Remember - 'failure' does not exist - it is merely an opportunity to learn, a stepping-stone to success. There is always a positive side.

For example, you could ask: What is brilliant about this setback/failure?

Answer: Absolutely nothing!
Ask it again

Answer: Well, I suppose I have discovered my biggest self-limiting belief.
Ask it again

Answer: It gives me time to reflect on what I am and am not good at.
Ask it again

Answer: It will help me to meet someone who can help and guide me.
Ask it again

Answer: It is giving me the opportunity to realise I have resources that I have never even used.

NOW - use this as a stepping-stone for your next move.

Turn your fear into excitement!

'I really want to but something is stopping me!' What is it? - **Fear!**

Fear arises as a feeling we might fail or that we might be rejected in some way and it all tends to happen in our imagination. We project the 'terrible event' into the future.

Here are two ways we can choose to respond to fear.

1. Use the energy
At times of crisis we are always more creative. Our minds are sharper and we remember things normally forgotten. We can run faster and further and go without sleep for long periods of time. One actor can be paralysed by fear before a performance to such a degree that he forgets his lines, while another can see the fear as excitement and use it to rise to hitherto unknown levels of creative expression.

Have you ever left your purse in a shop and then found yourself running at the most incredible speed to get back there? Or maybe you have had to get someone to hospital and found your driving skills increased dramatically? We can use the discomfort of fear as a driving force to do things that we would normally consider to be impossible. This enables us to tap into an immense potential of power that normally lies dormant within us.

2. Face your fear

The fear is always far worse than the thing we are afraid of and fear thrives on projections like, 'Oh my God, if I do this, such and such will happen...' While on Eurowalk we heard a story about a young boy who had just passed his driving test and it perfectly illustrates this point.

His father was so proud of him that he gave him the keys of his most prized possession - his vintage Mercedes - and told him to drive to the garage to put petrol in it.

'Fill up the tank, son,' he said. The boy was thrilled and terrified at the same time. He was so nervous, in fact, that he smashed the wing of the car as he drove out of the garage. He got out and looked at the damage while the fear of what his father would do to him began to take a firm hold. The car was his father's life! Should he run away from home? Or run away with the car? Perhaps he should commit suicide? These and many crazy thoughts went through his head as he wrestled with his fear.

Eventually he decided to face the music and tell his father. He stood quietly, trembling from head to toe as his father walked round the car, surveying the damage to his 'life'. He walked slowly and deliberately, his hands in his pockets, his brow furrowed in deep thought. He looked at his son, stretched out his hand and said, 'Well, son, the only thing left to do is to go back and fill her up again!'

 Facing your fear is a lot less lethal than your projection!

This technique cannot fail!

Draw up a chart like the one below, putting a cross in the left-hand column. Fill in the right-hand column making sure **never to make an entry on the left.**

✓ First write down your goal.

✓ Fill in the right column ONLY.

✓ **Put into action** everything you have written - **in the right order.**

Reasons I cannot achieve this	Ideas for how I can Succeed

I deserve to succeed

Do affirmations work? Well the negative ones have worked really well, haven't they? If one thought like, '**I can't have what I want**' can sabotage your whole life, imagine what the thought, '**I can have whatever I want**' could do!

Affirmation is basically internal communication.

People like Elvis Presley, Marilyn Monroe and Jimi Hendrix were brilliant at communicating their greatness to the world, but they had not learned how to communicate well internally. Their message to themselves was their downfall.

 Make your internal dialogue positive - talk to yourself nicely!

Action plan - the 'I deserve' breath

1. Sit comfortably with a straight spine, palms facing up, on knees.

2. Extend your tongue and fold the sides to form a narrow tube.

3. Inhale slowly and deeply through your folded tongue.
Use the full breath (page 199) to perform this exercise.

4. Relax the tongue to its natural position. Close the mouth and breathe out slowly through your nose.

This breath allows a free flow of energy through the body and purifies the mind, releasing any guilt.

Three Golden Rules of Affirmation

The magic of affirmation is the **practical approach** to it. When you engage your **whole self** and **your senses** in the process - **it will really work.**

1. Each time you repeat your affirmation, say it with a **deeper resonance**. Say it out loud at first, then softly, then in a whisper, then internally without sound. Each time you repeat the affirmation, go deeper into yourself and **make it profound**.

Or you could do it the other way round and repeat it internally, then in a whisper, louder and then a shout!

Repetition is the mother of success.

- Mansukh

2. Focus on the colours around you. As you repeat the sounds, increase the depth of colour. See your clothes change, feel the variety, tone and vibrant colour of everything around you.

3. Put emphasis at the right place - at the right pace - with **full concentration,** for example - I am **happy** - I **am** happy - **I** am happy.

Affirmations work!
Practise them until you become aware of the changes
they are creating. Then you will see it for yourself!

Never give up!

These three words sum up the power behind some of the greatest achievers in history. They are three of the most powerful words we know that have made a difference to thousands of people's lives.

The great freedom fighter, Mahatma Gandhi, achieved so much in his life because no matter how many circumstances turned against him, he **never gave up**. He anchored his determination never to give up by using a series of simple hand gestures.

We now offer you this same simple method as a means to change your destiny. It will clear the heaviness of disappointment and failure into determination to get up, try again and succeed!

Action plan

The Success Sequence - for making Success out of Failure

1. Stand up straight and bring your hands together in front of you at the level of the abdomen. Gesture: Allow the little finger tips of both hands to touch.

2. Breathe in and raise your hands up to the level of the navel.
Gesture: Allow ring fingers to touch as well. Breathe out.

3. Breathe in and raise the hands to heart level Gesture: Release the little and ring fingers and join the middle fingers. Breathe out.

4

4. Breathe in and turn the palms to face outwards, middle fingers still touching. Breathe out.

5

5. Breathe in and raise the arms up above the head turning the palms to face towards the ceiling. Breathe out.

6

6. Breathe in.
Gesture:
Now join thumb and index fingers together as well. Hands turn to face forwards. Breathe out.

7

7. Breathe in and imagine you are gently drawing a golden thread over your head with your fingers and thumbs to a distance of about a shoulder width.

8. As you breathe out, lower the hands slowly to shoulder level keeping them a shoulder's width apart. Gesture: At the same time let go the index fingers and allow the middle fingers to make contact with the thumbs.

8

10 - 11

10. Breathe in and as you breathe out lower to abdomen level. Gesture: Change the fingers so that now the little fingers and thumbs touch.

11. Breathing normally, place hands together, palms facing up, still holding the gesture.

9. Breathe in and allow the hands to continue to float down to the level of the heart as you breathe out. Gesture: change the fingers again so that ring fingers and thumbs touch.

9

231

12. Turn the hands over so that palms face towards the floor.

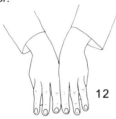

12

14. Still holding the gesture, place the palms together at the heart. Hold, and then focus on your breath for a few moments. Feel the power of stillness the sequence has created within you.

13. Breathe in and as you breathe out, turn the gesture inwards towards your body in a circular motion. Describe a full circle.

13

14

What we need is more people
who specialise in the impossible.
- Theodore Roethke

Eurowalk - Dingle Bay

233

Take control of the mind

All the obstacles to success arise in the mind which houses our thoughts.
By controlling the breath we can control the mind.

Indigenous cultures have kept their traditions intact by using breathing
techniques such as the ones that follow.

They have the power to change your whole experience of life,
transforming into success emotional obstacles such as guilt, fear, anxiety,
apathy, self doubt **and** fear of failure.

 The power of your life lies in your breath.

Action plan

Freedom from Fear Breath - This breath calms the mind, soothes the nervous system and releases the fear of failure.

> *Sit in a comfortable position.*
> *Fold your tongue back so that the underside is pressed against the top of your mouth.*
> *Breathe deeply and softly making a sound like that of someone in a deep sleep, or a sleeping baby.*
>
> ***Perform for about five minutes.***

Action plan

The Pro-active Breath

This breathing technique dispels apathy and laziness, activating the solar energy in the body.

1. Sit comfortably with your spine straight. Close your eyes to prepare your mind and just focus on your breath for a few minutes.

2. Raise your right hand and place your thumb on the right nostril. Middle and index fingers rest on the space between the eyebrows.

3. Close the left nostril with the ring finger and breathe out through the right nostril. Breathe in through the right again keeping the left closed. Continue in this way for about 15 breaths.

The ultimate success mantra

Turning Forty - Healing the Mid-life Crisis

Jeanne Katz

Leo Finkelstein

The Decade of Opportunity

*I*t doesn't usually feel like a time of great opportunity, does it? In fact, people often experience a kind of panic as they rush to fulfil all the dreams they had hoped to achieve.

In teaching medical professionals we have found countless forty year old consultants who have reached the pinnacle of their profession, only to find themselves looking forward to the future with the thought, 'Another twenty five years of this?'

Is there an answer? Of course there is, as most fifty year olds will tell you as they look back on their forties. The unrest of the forties makes us face, accept and finally appreciate ourselves as we truly are. As forty year olds we become forty year youngs as we take up the challenge and begin to search for answers.

 Life really can begin at forty.

239

What's happening? Is it all too late? Why do I feel so strange?

Very few of us are prepared for what will happen to us in the forties. It can come as a shock! In our thirties we have been used to being attractive and in our prime, at the peak of our energy, and all of a sudden our youthful good looks have begun to wane. One of the women attending a 'Women's Health' weekend commented:

One of the biggest shocks for me was standing in the supermarket one day and realising that the young men in their thirties no longer seemed to notice me, but older, more mature men did! Am I over the hill?

Although we are obviously getting older on the outside, inside we feel the same, youthful self and it can take a few years to come to terms with this sudden loss of youth and to accept the onset of maturity. We may start to panic inside if our self-esteem is based on the way we look and how attractive we may be to others.

Being forty years old is the greatest opportunity there is for becoming forty years young.

The grand review

Prepare yourself!
As we approach our forties everything seems to happen at once.
Children grow up and leave, our relationships can become strained and
health can begin to suffer if we haven't really looked after ourselves well
enough.

It is a time to review everything. Your relationship with yourself,
partner, children, career and your body all need looking at.

Take time out for YOU. Put YOU first. It's not selfishness, but self-
responsibility. If you don't look after yourself - who will? Remember
there are 1,440 minutes in a day. You owe at least 40 minutes for
yourself each day.

 **Make the changes work *for* you and
not *against* you.**

Healing the mid-life crisis

What is the so-called mid-life crisis? The dictionary defines the word 'crisis' as 'a turning point' and whatever happens to us we always have the choice to see it in this way.

Materialism has offered us so much and it's not until now that we begin to realise how unfulfilling it all can be, because **feelings are born from the inside** and not the outside. If we have opted for the comfort zone and things in life have not matched up to their original promise or expectations, at this point in our life we will be forced to **turn within** and ask ourselves several important questions.

The main questions that raise themselves are, 'Am I living the life I really want to live?' 'Am I being the person I really want to be?' This is really a **re-identity crisis** and the main issue that confronts us is the relationship we have with ourselves.

Healing the past

So many things have happened to us so far and many of these experiences may have been very painful but if we haven't managed to resolve the hurt, suppressing it all as a means of coping, it will tend to raise its lovely head in this decade!

The life events that happen around us merely act as triggers to the reservoir of unresolved issues: things like bereavement, relationship troubles, loss of a job or financial difficulties. It's important to see whatever happens as a *healing crisis* rather than a catastrophe. Don't worry! Once you are prepared, you can meet it all with a positive attitude.

Having said that, attitude is a great start, but it's not everything. You will also need the emotional energy to cope with it plus **good techniques,** skill, and positive expectations and **beliefs.**

Helena in India, 1997, with a family of four generations

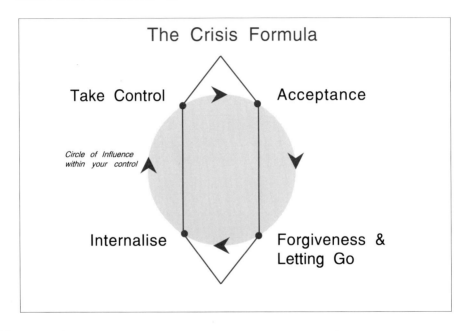

The Crisis Formula

Take Control

Acceptance

Circle of Influence
within your control

Internalise

Forgiveness &
Letting Go

The Crisis Formula

Crisis and suffering can become a catalyst for making change and for transforming ourselves in fundamental ways. It is life's way of getting our attention. Nothing ever happens by accident and there is always a very good reason for it.

Certain lessons will keep repeating themselves until we have learned what we are meant to and become what we are meant to be. If you find yourself in this position, however painful or uncertain it may feel, the opportunity is there to walk back into a life that is more satisfying than you ever thought possible. You just have to decide to make it work **for you** instead of **against you.**

 Remember - life is always leading you and never misleading you.

247

Face to face with crisis

One of the most important things that happened to me this year on Eurowalk 2000 was a meeting with a man called James Everett in prison. He had been there for fifteen years as part of a life sentence.

Involved in a robbery that went wrong James gave himself up when he discovered that a man had been tragically and mistakenly killed during the robbery. Faced by crisis on a grand scale, James has triumphed over it in the most incredible way and become a source of inspiration to hundreds of people in the process.

When he first arrived in prison he was very shocked by the unnatural and alien environment. In this letter written from his prison cell, he described to me how it felt.

- Mansukh

The darkest hour

This was to be the darkest and most painful period of my life. I had great difficulty dealing with the reality of the crime, its consequences, and the pain and destruction I had caused so many people. It was too big, too enormous for me to deal with.

At my lowest point I sat down and planned with determined effort how I was going to take my own life.

Then I said to myself, 'Give me one good reason why you should not see this through!'

A noticeable quiet and calm presence pervaded the room. Beyond the chaos and turbulence of my mind something deep within me was making itself known.

It was as if there was something deep within my heart vibrating, like a seed of light, very still, yet pulsating. That 'something' was offering me acceptance of my flaws and inadequacies.

The feeling became stronger. I fell to the floor and began to sob deeply. The deeper I cried the stronger the feeling became.

Within all the darkness and negativity something within me existed which was good and loving, accepting me, urging me to surrender to it, to give in to it.

During that night I cried for hours. I realised that my life had been one of attempting to live up to the expectations of others, desperately trying to seek approval and recognition from people to feel whole and complete.

This letter from James moved me so much that I knew the
crisis of his life could become an inspiration to thousands of
people. Combining our skills and wisdom we present
The Crisis Formula.

Please use it because it comes from a man who, still in
prison, is sharing his deepest insights with you.

1 *Take control*

In the prison, James began to take control of his situation.
He didn't blame anyone else for what had happened, because he knew
that he was completely responsible for his predicament. This is the first
step in dealing with any crisis situation. It is very important not to blame
anyone else for what is happening to you, but to take the situation into
your own hands. **Take control.**

Every day ask yourself three times:

1. Why is this happening to me?
2. What do I need to learn from this?
3. What do I need to change in my approach to life?

Write down any answers that come to you. You will be amazed what
your heart/body/mind consciousness will tell you if you ask the right
questions.

*Over the next four years with the guidance and love of a counsellor
trained in psychology, my yoga teacher and the support of family and
friends, I began a journey of discovery and self-growth. The path has
not been without struggle and the transition has not happened overnight.*

But let me tell you that this struggle shines out of his eyes. Moving on to
the next stage of our formula ...

*I realised that although I could not change what I had done, or the fact
that I was in prison, I could change who I was and potentially what I
would become. Just because I was in prison did not mean my life had
to stop. Symbolically, that night a large part of me died, and from
within I was offered a way forward.*

James' next step was to accept what he could not change.

2 *Acceptance*

There is a constant dance between acceptance and making changes. Things happen in life that we have absolutely no control over. People we love can die, suffer illness or disability and we can lose our job or be let down by people we trusted. So many things are beyond our control, but the pain we feel comes from the fact that we **just cannot accept** what has happened.

This prayer which I found in the halls at Bangor University, will help to start you off on the journey of acceptance.

- *Mansukh*

The Serenity Prayer

God grant me the serenity to
accept the things I cannot
change,
the courage to change the
things I can and
the wisdom to know the
difference.

255

What have I got to accept?

Everything! Especially the things you perceive as negative. HOW?

Is your identity tied up with parenting? It may be time to change your identity. Are your children growing up and moving away? Let them go. They are setting you free to pursue new things. Someone once sent me a card on which these words were written

If you love something let it go
If it comes back it is yours
If not, it never was

The days of youth are behind us and our physical looks are changing. If self-esteem is tied up with how attractive we are its definitely time to build self-worth on deeper, more mature values.

The Gesture of Acceptance

With the right index finger touching the left thumb, take hold of middle, ring and little fingers of the right hand with the four remaining fingers of the left hand.

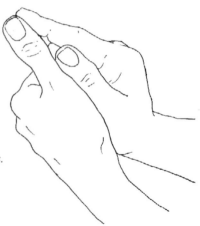

Hold the hands with fingers pointing upwards. Hold for at least sixty to ninety seconds.

Affirm: I accept what I cannot change.

257

Can things really get worse?

No sooner had James come to terms with the overwhelming crisis of having to spend his life in prison, than he had to face another, even greater one. He could never have anticipated that his relationship of almost a decade and a half was about to end. His wife, unable to wait for him, had decided to live with another man. This event would not only affect his remaining life but the lives of his two beautiful children.

This is his heart-rending account.

As much as I tried to embrace the pain, it was tearing me apart. My future, and security while in prison, seemed to have been sucked into a void of futility.

One evening I was talking with a friend who had been in prison for some twenty years. He could see and sense my confusion and despair.
'Do you love her?' he asked me.
'Of course I do!' I said.
'Then let her go,' he said.
'I have let her go!' I replied enraged by his remark.
'No you haven't,' he said, 'because if you truly love her and want her to be happy, you would be pleased to let her go as a gift from you and your heart, with your blessing.'

As his words filtered through the miasma of pain in my mind I picked up the cup of tea he had made for me. It was boiling hot and the cup had no handle. It burnt my hand and I had to let it go. It dropped on to the floor.

Slowly recognition came to me. That was what I was doing - emotionally holding on to the pain and the situation instead of letting go of it. In fact, by holding on to her, I was only hurting myself. I began to cry and realised that she really did deserve to be happy and in a deeper way, it would make me happy too.

As I felt the reality of this insight a wave of joy and relief flowed up from my heart and throughout my whole body.

I felt a deep sense of peace as if I had let go of a great weight.

James had to learn the power of forgiveness and letting go. I believe that during this transition period, he was experiencing the depth and strength of his own ability to forgive and the freedom that comes from letting go.

2 *Forgiveness and letting go*

The power of healing any crisis in the forties lies in our ability to transform any event into a storehouse of good, useable energy. What does that mean? It means using the power of positive forgiveness.

Forgiveness is one of the key factors in recovery.

We must be able to forgive others for anything they may have done to us.

Forgiveness is an act of courage and strength. You are daring to accept and do those things that other people simply aren't even willing to try. Those who forgive are the ones who win.

 Life is an exciting adventure when you are willing to forgive.

261

Forgiveness asks us to look at everything that has ever happened that may be stopping us from moving forward.

✓ **Look for the good points** in the person or situation that has hurt you.

✓ **Ask yourself:** 'What is brilliant about this?' Your mind will always say 'nothing' at first. Persevere until you find something, even if it is that it has taught you how not to behave.

✓ **Go to a river.** Pick up a stick and as you hold it, place all your feelings of anger, resentment, bitterness and rage into it and then throw it into the river. (Just a little stick!)

Or if you want to be really dramatic, you could emulate the old American Indians and dig a hole in the ground, put your head into it and speak (or shout) all your old feelings into it. Go for it - but don't forget to cover it up again!

 If you have never talked to anyone about the way you feel, find someone who will listen without judgement and tell them. If all else fails, talk to the mirror, your poodle or even the goldfish!

 If the person who has hurt you has died, plant a tree in their name as an offering of forgiveness. As you plant it, wish them well on their journey and consciously let go of any negative connection you have had with them.

 Remember that forgiveness can be fun and creative - it doesn't have to be filled with doom and gloom!

The Gesture of Forgiveness

1. Clasp your hands together in front of you at chest level.

2. Breathe in, and raise them above your head. Breathe out and hold your hands in the air.

Affirm: *I forgive and let go of the past.*

3. Release.

Repeat with the opposite hand-hold.

Be the first to forgive
to smile and take the first step
And your will see happiness bloom
On the face of your human brother or sister.

Be always the first
Do not wait for others to forgive
For by forgiving you become the master of fate
The fashioner of life, the doer of miracles.

To forgive is the highest most beautiful form of love.

In return you will receive
untold peace and happiness.

- Robert Muller

265

Action plan - Forgiveness and letting go

Stop for a moment and close your eyes (after you have read this!)

Imagine yourself very free inside from any hurt or chaos.

Feel it now.

Stand up as if you loved and liked everybody in your life.

How does it feel?

As you stand there, visualise yourself full of strength and power and then say out loud:

It is time to.....

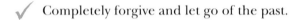 Completely forgive and let go of the past.

Forgive and accept myself and everything about who I am.

Let go of the old me and move into what I have become.

Let go and clear unresolved pain so that I can move forward.

It is a time for maturity in thought and emotion, a time to forgive and have fun!

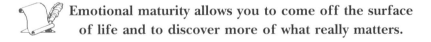 **Emotional maturity allows you to come off the surface of life and to discover more of what really matters.**

The Gesture of Letting Go

1. Stand tall and straight with your eyes closed. Think about an event or incident in your life that you want to let go of.

3. Palms facing down, breathe out as you bring your hands down in front of face to level of the abdomen.

2. Breathing in, raise your arms to the sides and up above your head.

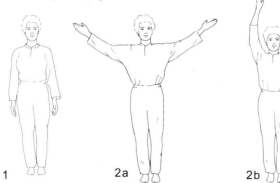

1　　　　　　2a　　　　　　2b　　　　　3

4. Slowly push hands away from the body ten inches apart, until stretched out in front. Slowly relax elbows, turn palms towards you.

5. Bending elbows on the outbreath draw hands towards the face and either side of the head, pushing the memory back behind your head.

6. Turn palms to face outward and push them forward, breathing in.

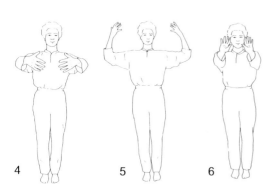

4   5   6

7. Turn palms inward and on the outbreath draw them back towards your face and either side of the head again, pushing the memory even further behind you

Affirm: *I am letting go of the past. It cannot touch me.*

8. Repeat this movement many times, each time pushing the memory further behind you, until it becomes a little dot in the distance.

Dealing with the emotions

Crisis is often a time for 'emotional commotion'. We need to be able to find creative outlets for all the different feelings that emerge during this time.

James has become a master at letting go of emotions. He found that yoga and meditation were a perfect way to balance and work with all the challenges of being in prison. He has also discovered that in working with his emotions positively, a powerful, creative energy has been released within him. In his letter he explained.

Acting is ideal, as I found it to be an immediate form of expression. It gave me a creative arena where I could express and explore my experiences, my pain and the whole range of human emotions in a positive, constructive way.

Action plan

Learn to allow any feelings to emerge, whatever they may be - guilt, fear, anger, sorrow, disappointments, insecurity - and play them out if you have to.

You could be outrageous!

If you always wanted to go break dancing - **do it now.**
If you always wanted to learn to play the flute - **do it now.**
If you always wanted to go skiing, play football, roller blading, watch a Walt Disney film, white water rafting, parachuting - **do it now!**

They may be the only moments you will remember when you look back on your life.

They are ways in which you can learn to love yourself no matter what you are feeling and **it's the best thing you will *ever do!***

The power of inner healing

Imagine teaching yoga in prison to people who are aggressive and violent. James has witnessed many miracles since he began to share what he has learned with the other prisoners. He told me one story about someone who we will call Joe, who had been in and out of prison all his life.

Renowned for his hardness and ability to inflict intense physical pain on people who stood in his way, Joe was serving seven years for armed robbery and grievous bodily harm.

His face was etched with pain, he couldn't sleep, he was deeply hostile to everyone and complained of not being able to relax and having bouts of paranoia. He tentatively approached me about the prison yoga class I was teaching and then reluctantly turned up with two other inmates. I found out later that he had actually threatened other people with violence if they came along.

We started off with relaxation and deep breathing and I noticed his face started to twitch. He had so much tension in his body that he could hardly breathe at all and I was concerned for him. I explained the notion of needing to let go, and compared it to the hard man image we use to protect ourselves in prison. I could see he was absorbing what I was saying.

After an hour of posture work I talked them through a Vipassana meditation and then his whole body began to visibly shake as a lot of energy started to be released. At the end everyone left except Joe who sat rigidly cross-legged, his whole body shaking uncontrollably. When I asked him if he was alright he opened his eyes and looked at me and then a huge wave of emotion erupted out of his body.

He collapsed on the floor, sobbing and crying while intermittently apologising for this display of emotion.

He eventually shared his life story with me.

It was a pitiful history of child abuse, violence and total disconnection from his emotions. His belief that he was unlovable and unworthy of love poured out of him in garbled, incoherent ramblings.

He was releasing a past that had been trapped inside him for years.

Over the next few weeks the change in him was astounding. He even became much more relaxed, looked fifteen years younger and started to smile! Today he is out of prison and has settled down and married. He runs his own garage and tells me that he meditates every day.

The Sequence of Inner Healing

This sequence allows us to let go of sadness and grief and to heal the wounds of the past.

1. Standing straight and tall, cross your arms right over left in front of you.

2. Breathe in and slowly draw the arms up in front as if taking off a jumper.

3. Turn hands to face outwards and gently start to lower the arms.

1   2   3

The Sequence of Inner Healing

4. At shoulder height with palms facing forward, flick the wrists once in a circular motion.

6.Continuing the outbreath perform one more wrist flick at the level of the navel.

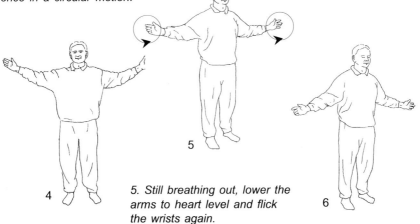

4

5

5. Still breathing out, lower the arms to heart level and flick the wrists again.

6

4 *Internalise*

James told me that he is convinced that the only place real healing can come from is deep within ourselves. 'When we can hand over our crisis to a greater power,' he said, 'and then learn to trust it, something very magical begins to happen.'

It is interesting that the third step in the A.A.'s successful **Twelve Step Programme** is to be willing to ask God for help - to hand the problem over to something greater than ourselves. When we can start to really trust that power and believe it exists, life can become quite fascinating. James found it transforming.

During my long periods of solitary confinement which were often for twenty to twenty four hours a day, I discovered I was not alone. I became aware of an incredible force of love guiding and assisting me - all the time.

Long hours of solitary enabled me to strengthen and renew my inner connection and to form a deeper union with that place in my heart where unconditional love and peace reside. The stiller my mind becomes the more this connection is given life.

I have realised that I am not alone any more, just struggling to survive, and that now I can trust the process of change. I know it will always see me through to the most perfect conclusion.

The crisis of my life has really changed me and I am now more fulfilled as a human being than I could ever have imagined possible.

For the past year and a half I have been teaching yoga, meditation and stress management workshops in conjunction with probation officers and drug counsellors. So far, I have worked with over 500 people, staff and inmates alike.

My journey of the past fifteen years has given me the chance to reconcile myself with a destructive past and an opportunity to give and share with others. Love, yoga and art nourish my existence, giving me hope and sustenance and a love for life which enables me to transcend the limitations of the sentence I am serving.

What most people call a 'painful death' for the caterpillar, is actually the birth of a beautiful butterfly.....

- *Mansukh*

279

Action plan

The Internalising Gesture

Perform The Gesture of Peace (Page 144) using only the first affirmation. Focus your mind on the ground and count up to twenty-five breaths.

1. Sit comfortably with your back as straight as possible.

2. Inhale slowly and deeply. Close your ears with your thumbs. Then place your index fingers over your eyes and middle fingers against the nostrils. The ring and little fingers are placed above and below the lips to close the mouth.

Feel your awareness draw to a point directly in the centre of your head as if the eyes and ears were at a distance.

James Everett is a perfect example of what you can do when you put into action what you know and place all your energy behind it. In life there is no down that cannot be brought up, no crisis that cannot be healed.

There is never a moment when the power of the human spirit is weaker than the predicament we face. Adversity and crisis allow that light to shine so that we can find the miracle.

What lies behind us and what lies before us are tiny matters compared to what lies within us.

- Ralph Waldo Emerson

Approaching Fifty

Tilly, Margaret and Nan / Pathfinders Course, North Wales

Approaching Fifty -
The Gateway to Second Adulthood

*A*s we approach our fiftieth year we are actually passing through the gateway to our second adulthood. With all the growth and transformation of the forties it may be a bit of a tight squeeze, but our maturity will see us through! Maturity brings a fresh perspective which allows us to discover one of the greatest treasures there is in life - that the **key to happiness** and **success** in life is **within us.**

It all depends on our ability to bring it out and share it with the world.

If you have managed to use your early forties well, you will have transformed a lot of the **energy** of the past and will feel alive, vibrant and ready to go.

What do I do with the rest of my life?

Derek is a dear friend who exemplifies the 'get up and go' of the fifties. Today he is teaching yoga and inspiring many people with his zest and enthusiasm for life.

I was just approaching the high point of my professional and business life. My career had spanned over 35 years with a well-known pharmaceutical company.

I remember in vivid detail going into my office very early one summer morning to deal with a backlog of problems. As I sat down at my desk I paused to look out of the window, and saw that a glorious sunrise had painted the sky with a breathtaking palette of beautiful colours.

*The extraordinary clarity of that sky triggered a simple but crucial question in my mind ....
'What am I about to do with my remaining life?'*

It was such a persistent question, that I couldn't wait for the energy to dissipate. Before the same sun had set, I had put into motion a process that was to lead to an early, successful and adventurous retirement.

Derek Budge – Advanced Dru Yoga

285

This is the decade for expansion and fulfilment

How come? For most of our life we can focus our attention on what we want to achieve from all our efforts and strivings, but in the late forties we begin to realise that **something needs to change.**

Often crisis in the forties can bring us to the point where we realise that we need to think carefully about the rest our life and what we can do that will **benefit the lives of others.**

Turning fifty we find ourselves with a new-found freedom and a rekindled sense of adventure. This is the time of the eminent leader, post-menopausal zest, a new willingness to stand up and be counted for who you are **and** what you believe in.

The importance of service

Audrey is one of the most special people we know. She joined our yoga course whilst in her fifties and during one weekend of the course I talked about the importance of feeding people. No sooner had she arrived back in her home town than she rang up the local organisation concerned with feeding the homeless and they allocated her a Friday night slot.

- Mansukh

That Friday I started preparing soup and sandwiches for the seventy or more homeless people. Since then I have joined forces with a friend and now we have five teams of helpers from among our yoga students. They also collect clothes, blankets, socks and gloves to give out on Friday nights.

Some of the people we serve food to are very desperate and we come across all sorts of situations. We know that we are fulfilling a great need by giving them the feeling that someone really does care and it is such a joy to be able to help them.

It can also be a lot of fun. The other week it was pouring with rain so we all wore plastic bags on our heads, including the homeless people! One of our helpers had her six-year-old son with her. He loved every minute of it.

I have found that if I need any help, I just have to ask. Last week, in just three days, we gathered a bed, mattress, pillows, duvet and covers, pots, pans and kitchen utensils, bed linen, plates, cups and a microwave for a young man who had just been allocated a flat. In reality people are so willing to give. All I have done is to provide them with an opportunity. The human heart is so open and, in truth, we all have such a great longing to help each other.

- Audrey

Scottish Retreat, 1996

That I feed the hungry,
forgive an insult, and love my enemy -
these are great virtues.
But what if I should discover
that the poorest of the beggars
and most impudent of offenders
are all within me,
and that I stand in need
of the alms of my own kindness;
that I myself am the enemy
who must be loved -
what then?

- Carl Jung

Have a look round and see what you can do

Mahatma Gandhi was forty-six when he arrived back in India to start again from scratch after successfully ending ethnic oppression of Asians in South Africa. He could easily have become a successful barrister again, but instead he travelled around India for a year observing the Indian people and discovering how best he could help them.

From then on he made his life a near-perfect example of how giving creatively, in whatever way you can, leads to ultimate peace and contentment.

One day, as Gandhi was boarding a train, one of his sandals fell off onto the track and, as the train was already moving, he couldn't retrieve it. He immediately threw his other sandal onto the track in the same place. Asked why, he explained, 'At least the poor fellow who finds them will have a pair to wear now.'

Sing your own song

Many times people simply don't believe they have anything to offer.

But the decade of the fifties is often full of **life, vitality and energy**. As we enter our second adulthood we need to recognise that we have all the strength, experience and ability that is necessary to find our own song and sing it out loud!

Talking of singing reminds me of the time Eurowalk 2000 went to Bosnia and visited the beautiful village of Medugorje. It was there that I heard a nightingale sing for the first time. I couldn't believe that such a tiny bird could make such an exquisite sound.

It sang all night long and when we woke up in the morning, it was still singing. It reminded me of this poem by Saint Francis.

- Mansukh

Oh little brother bird that singest with full heart
And having nought possesses all
Surely thou dost well to sing!
For thou hast life without labour and beauty without burden
And riches without care.
When thou wakest, lo, it is dawn.
And when thou comest to sleep it is eve.
And when thy two wings lie folded about thy heart
Lo, there is rest.
Therefore sing, brother, having this great wealth
That when thou singest thou givest thy riches to all!

St. Francis of Assisi

Elspeth and Lilly - International Health Conference, North Wales

What am I most concerned about?

Start by asking yourself, 'What means more to me than anything else?' and 'What has my life's experience shown me?' **Think about it for a moment.**

Perhaps a relative or friend has suffered from a particular disease and you would like to support the medical research in that area. You may feel deeply about the destruction of the rain forests or the killing of baby seals or dolphins.

Write down on a piece of paper, '**What means more to me than anything else in the world is ....'**

It may be only one thing or it may be several. Which feels most significant? Which one brings a surge of energy or excitement?

Every little counts

If you ever find yourself thinking that you have nothing to offer, think about this story that I often share with my children.

The forest was on fire! The little parrot wanted desperately to help. Seeing a stream nearby he flew down and dipped his tiny wings into the water and then flew up above the flames and shook them. He flew back and forth from the stream to the fire over and over again, oblivious to the searing heat and his own exhaustion.

Looking down on the little parrot, the Gods were amused. They laughed and said, 'What does he think he's doing? What difference will a few drops of water make?'

The parrot thought to himself, 'As long as I can fly, I will never give up.' The flames climbed higher and higher and scorched his wings and then the God of Compassion felt sorry for him. He took on the form of a golden eagle and flew down to tell the parrot to give up and save himself. 'Those little drops of water cannot make any difference,' he said to him.

'Don't tell me to stop!' said the parrot. 'Why don't you help me instead? I will never give up.' The eagle was very moved by the valiant efforts of the little bird, so much so that huge golden tears began to fall from his eyes. They were so huge that they put out the fire!

'That's more like it!' gasped the parrot. 'Please don't stop!' he said as he fell to the ground burnt and dying. The eagle's heart burst open at the sight and his tears brought all the animals and trees back to life - including the little parrot.

- Mansukh

297

I am only one; but still I am one.
I cannot do everything, but still I can do something.
I will not refuse to do the something I can do.

- Helen Keller

Action plan

Heaven and Earth Sequence -
to connect with your inner qualities

1. Begin with hands at heart level six inches apart and facing each other - fingers relaxed.

2. Breathe in, raise the right hand whilst lowering the left hand until the heel of the right hand is stretched up and the left down.

3. Breathe out - relax and bring the arms to the starting point.

4. Breathe in - repeat with the left arm stretching up and the right down.

Repeat five to six times.

299

Everyone has something to give

Focus on the qualities **that you do have**. Everyone has something they are good at that makes them feel great.

Gandhi focused all his power and energy on one single thing - ahimsa, or **non-violence.** This was his greatest quality and strength and in offering it to benefit the world he discovered an indestructible force moving in his life. It was a force that brought freedom to India. Mother Teresa was forty-seven when she first knelt down to help a dying man in the streets of Calcutta. She also had one very powerful gift to offer - her compassionate, **never-ending care**.

Once again, she focused her whole life's work on that one quality and went on to create a miracle that has made her a living saint. She didn't even think or plan ahead, but simply cared for the first person she met, then the next, and the next.....

Maybe it's time to turn your life around

My professor at University was a wonderful man who, in his young days, was trained by Alexander Fleming and worked in the prestigious Louis Pasteur Institute in France. Well-known and respected in scientific circles, he was famous for his amazing discoveries in the field of biochemistry and was sometimes referred to as 'The Welsh Wizard.' By the time I concluded my doctorate, I was privileged enough to see him awarded the F.R.S., the scientific equivalent of the Nobel Peace Prize.

He spent a large part of his life using animals in bio-assays in his research to help humanity. While I was working with him we developed a system of working with blood samples and cultures to substantiate our research. This meant that we could get the results we needed without causing harm to the animals.

There were many memorable moments that made our journey together very significant for me, but two incidents stand out in my mind more than any others. The first was in his later years, when Professor Evans and his wife, Dr Antis Evans, had bought some land on the beautiful island of Anglesey. The land was almost barren, but before long we had planted trees and shrubs and created ponds which attracted many different kinds of wildlife to take shelter there.

They also converted two old derelict cottages, one of which was made into a research laboratory where children could come on field trips. What affected me most deeply was the fact that here was a man who had spent many years contributing to scientific research that had unfortunately involved the use of animal bio-assays. Now I was witnessing the same man saving and preserving animals' lives.

The second miraculous moment relates to the walnut grove that was planted on the reserve. For many years the trees never bore fruit. Then one year Professor Evans was found lying in the shade of the grove, motionless, without breath, surrounded by the plants and animals he loved. In his right hand, he held a walnut.

He died a fulfilled man, leaving an unforgettable legacy behind him - a man whose life had enriched the lives of hundreds of others. I hold onto the memory of this great man, tightly clutching the seed of life in his hand.

Late Professor W.C. Evans, F.R.S., U.C.N.W., Bangor

I can make a difference

In 1994 I was invited by Mansukh to go on a pilgrimage - not to Mecca, or Bethlehem or even Lourdes, but to Auschwitz.

For me it was a very personal mission and something which I felt very strongly about. It was part of a peace vigil set up to celebrate fifty years of freedom. Jews and Germans were gathering together to sing songs and light candles in order to forgive and heal the past.

When I arrived at the camp I felt strangely disconnected from it all and couldn't touch the feeling inside me that I had wanted to. All I could see was a barren piece of ground and empty barracks. I had heard all the gruesome stories and knew of the extent of the tragedies, but I couldn't feel anything. Late at night, lying awake in my hotel bedroom, I found myself unable to sleep. I felt confused and a little desperate. Why had I come to this strange place?

Then, in the dank silence of the musty Polish hotel I heard the faint but unmistakable sound of train wheels clattering across the railway sleepers. Something inside me shuddered and I sat bolt upright feeling suddenly shocked and alarmed. 'My God!' I thought, 'that is the railway track that brought thousands of people to their deaths.'

I realised that it was this very sound that must have been heard by so many frightened people, over and over again. Something hit home and a great surge of feeling rose up inside me in that moment. 'It must never, ever happen again,' I said out loud - and I really meant it.

*There it was - the feeling I had been looking for! - that I must **believe** that my one life **could make a difference**, that my efforts, however small, could affect the future of the world.*

I strengthened my resolve to make sure that they did.

- Helena

Birkenau / Auschwitz II, Dec 199

Action plan

Pebble Visualisation Technique

Imagine as you approach the gateway to your second adulthood that you are standing at the edge of the sea. The great ocean is stretching out in front of you for miles. The sky is blue and the sun is shining as you look down and see a stone lying in the sand at your feet.

Pick it up. You are going to write on that stone the one quality you have to offer to the world. Think deeply. If there is more than one, bend down and pick up another stone and write on that too.

Now take each stone and hurl it out into the sea with **as much energy as you can.** Imagine as you do so that you are tapping into that quality of yours and offering it to the ocean of the world.

Now let's get practical

Once you have found out what you have to offer, what one action can you take **today** that will set it in motion?

Perhaps you can set up a meeting, be a chair-person, or offer money or administration skills. Maybe you would like to emulate Audrey and start a soup kitchen for the homeless. Remember she started by cooking soup at home and taking it out in her car.

Do it NOW!

Don't get distracted!

Shizo Kanakuri started his Olympic marathon in Stockholm in 1912 and after running a few miles was invited into someone's garden for a drink. He accepted because he was suffering from heat exhaustion.

Before he continued running on from the house, he caught a train to Stockholm, boarded a boat for Japan, got married and had six children and ten grandchildren. It was 1966 when, for the honour of Japan, he returned to the same garden to complete the marathon. It only took him 54 years!

Dealing with natural bodily changes

Uncomfortable bodily symptoms can be seen as a signal to push us towards our purpose in life. Either we can get absorbed and distracted by the discomforts or we can use them **to urge us on.**

Once I had discovered my purpose I found that the symptoms of menopause dramatically reduced and that, in fact, they were my signal to move into greater things.

Get it right and your energy will start to rise and expand into ......
.... The Free Flying Fifties!

- Helena

Menopause? I love it!

It was somewhere in my mid-forties that I began to realise that something was happening to me and, yes, perhaps this was **'The Change'**.

I knew it had to be something very important to warrant a capital 'C', although most of the women I knew seemed to be dreading it.

Not for the first time in my life, I decided to be different! Like many other changes I had been through I was determined to look forward and get excited by it. But it's difficult to get excited by a change if you don't know anything about it, isn't it?

So I started to read. The more I read, the more I got excited because it soon became clear to me that a whole world of approaches to the menopause existed that were simply not being offered to women.

Within six months I had amassed enough information to offer my first **'Menopause Matters'** workshop and the demand was electrifying. In two years I had travelled throughout the UK, the Netherlands and Belgium teaching nearly one thousand women how to handle the menopause.

Menopause had become my gift and the gateway to becoming a Woman of Wisdom.

It can become a gift for you too - if you let it. It can form your bridge between the child-bearing years and becoming a Woman of Wisdom. **Recognise the signs.** It's a time when you have to start to see that all the learning you have had up to now needs to be offered back as wisdom to the world.

 Menopause holds the potential for being the most transforming time of your life.

What are the opportunities?

If you find it difficult to get to grips with this phase in your life, take comfort from the fact that an understanding of what is happening to you not only eases the process, but actually helps you to **make the most of the changes** that are taking place.

Change is natural

Menopause, like birth, death and motherhood, is as normal and as natural as the changing seasons. As with any change in life, if we struggle and resist, it will be painful, but if we can flow *with* it, it can be easy and even beneficial. You can probably think of many occasions in your life when you've fought against changes, only to wonder what all the fuss was about once you have safely reached the other side!

1. Listen to your body

In the earlier stages, when hormone levels may be fluctuating wildly, you may well experience uncomfortable symptoms. Natural therapies will help to alleviate, or even avoid, the discomfort. **Listen carefully** to what your body and emotions are telling you and respond accordingly.

2. Adjust to your changing needs

For example, if your body starts to slow down naturally, why try to force yourself to lead a hectic lifestyle? **Take things a bit easier.**

If your eyesight sometimes lets you down, it may be a sign for you to **look inwards** more, so why not learn to meditate or do gentle yoga to balance the body and the mind? This will enhance your natural ability at this stage in life to be stronger and more settled within yourself and to feel content just to **be yourself.**

Post-menopausal zest

This is the really exciting bit because once you reach the later stages of menopause, the hormones come back into balance and all the energy that has been tied up in child-rearing is suddenly set free.

Margaret Meade, the well-known anthropologist, suffered many traumas in her forties, yet went on in her fifties to make stunning contributions to her field. 'There is no greater power on earth than the zest of a post-menopausal woman,' she concluded.

In my advertising literature I enjoy stating that I'm a grandmother about to turn fifty, celebrating the change in life and, like all great changes, you gain far more from the experience if you help others by teaching what you have learned.

'It's magic, absolutely magic,' wrote one participant recently. 'I no longer get angry or upset and appreciate every moment and experience. In the stillness of my mind I think I've found peace.' Yes, the menopause is like this. It can bring you peace.

Action plan

✓ **Read and learn** about the menopause.

✓ **Join a support group** where you can laugh and share experiences, or have a 'Menopause Party' yourself.

✓ **Tune into your body's changing needs**. Make more time for yourself.

✓ **Keep stress-free** and make time for creative and relaxing activities.

✓ **Reconnect with nature** - go for walks, work in the garden or with plants.

✓ **Complementary therapies** can help you adjust to the changes with minimum discomfort.

✓ **Tell other women** about the positive aspects of menopause.

Posture of Balance and Harmony

1. Sit on your heels placing hands on your knees.

2. Breathe in and raise your outstretched arms vertically above the head.

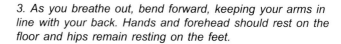

3. As you breathe out, bend forward, keeping your arms in line with your back. Hands and forehead should rest on the floor and hips remain resting on the feet.

4. Breathe evenly in this position.

5. Breathe in, let arms relax and slowly uncurl back to the starting position.

Cat/Tiger Sequence

Stage 1

1. Kneel on all fours, knees and hands a shoulder-width apart. Breathe in and lower the back as you raise the head and hips. Breathe out and repeat

2. Breathe in, and as you breathe out, tuck tailbone under, lower head and arch back.

Stage 2

1. Breathe in and lower
the back as before. Lift
the bent left leg until
thigh is parallel to the
floor.

1

2. Breathe out, arching the back upwards
- head comes down. Tuck left knee into
chest keeping foot off the floor.

2

Repeat with other leg.
Perform up to 3 times each side.

3. Relax in the Child Pose

3

What's going on for men?

Not to be outdone, you may, or may not, be pleased to know that there is a recognised 'male menopause' and it's called the andropause!

Firstly, recent research suggests that many men will experience a few years when hormones find new levels causing discomfort from many symptoms. It can be an enormous relief to know that you are not falling apart and that for the most part **these symptoms will pass!**

The fifties itch

What about relationship break-ups?
Fluctuating emotions and sexuality?
Staleness at work and home that leaves you feeling uncertain and out of control?

It is part of being male to want to be clear, strong, in control and certain you are heading in the right direction. At fifty many men are discovering a new and more tender side of themselves and wanting to explore and develop the experience of **'caring'.**

It can be very tempting at this age to find relief by re-living some of the wilder dreams of the teens or twenties in fast cars, fast yachts or fast relationships.

The fact that women in their twenties are naturally expressing their most tender and caring sides can make relationships with younger women very enticing.

It is rare, however, for these experiences to really provide the rich satisfaction and companionship that men of this age are searching for. There are two far more enduring solutions to 'the fifties itch'.

Action plan

✓ **Give your body space.** Keep yourself stress-free with regular exercise and make time to walk and camp in nature. If you find discomfort in energy levels, emotions or sexuality, complementary therapies can really help.

✓ **Look up and out, not in.** Yes, it can be tempting to retreat into a space where you just want excitement, comfort or love, but in the end almost all men will find the greatest rewards come not from looking in, but from looking out.

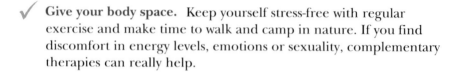 **Remember!**
This is the time to use your skills and talents for the benefit of the world.

Energy Shower

1. Stand with knees soft, back straight, arms relaxed by sides.

2.&3. Breathe in, raise the hands close to the body, palms uppermost until hands are at level of throat. Turn them over as hands raise above head until arms are outstretched, elbows soft, palms facing up.

1   2   3

4. Hold hands in this position visualising energy from the sun flowing into and filling an imaginary bowl in your hands.

5. Bend knees a little more, draw your hands over your head, palms facing down and slowly lower in front of your body. Imagine a shower of energy pouring down through your body and into the ground.

6. Return your hands to your sides.

Repeat as often as you like.

4

5

6

325

I don't know what your destiny may be,
but one thing I know. The only ones among you
who will be really happy are those
who have sought and found how to serve.

- Albert Schweitzer

Topusko, Bosnia 1996

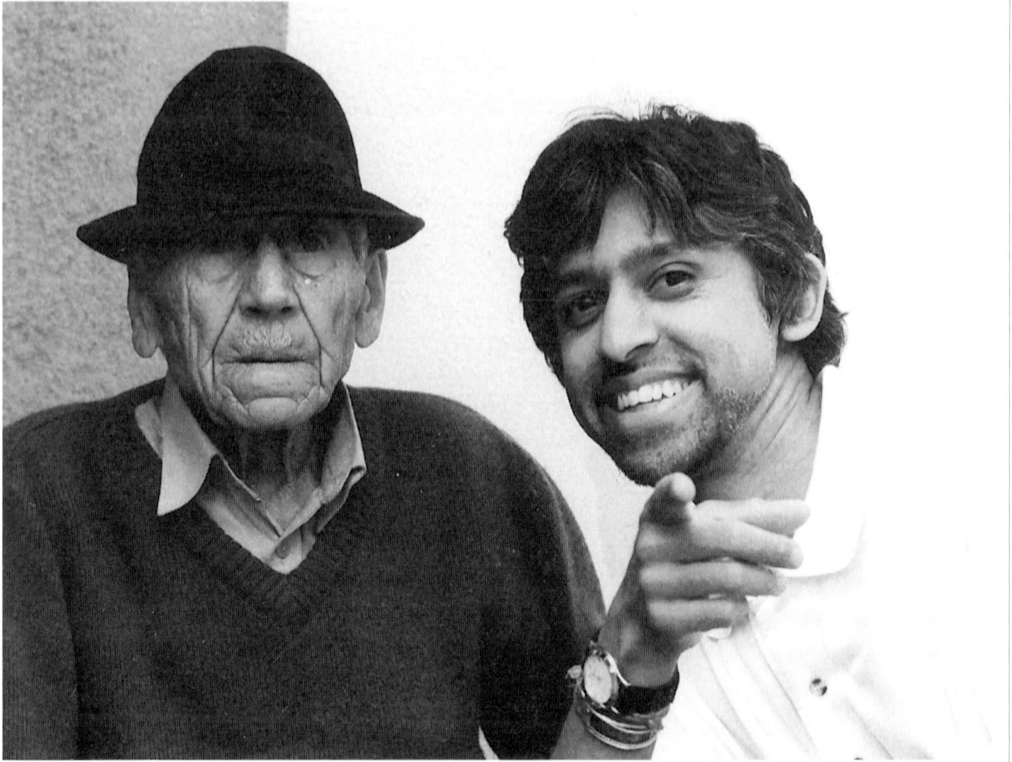

Growing Old Gracefully

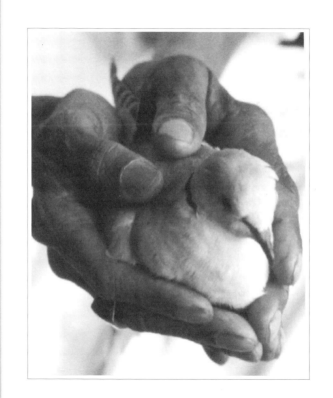

We older folk are worth a fortune
with silver in our hair
gold in our teeth
gas in our stomachs
stones in our kidneys and lead in our feet

Although I have aged a little since last we met
I am quite a lively old girl
With two old men who never leave me alone

One is Arthur Ritus who is with me all the time
The other is Will Power who gets me out of bed

- Anon

329

*I*n many cultures old age is something to be looked forward to with anticipation. It is a time when people become the **Wise Elders** of the community and are **respected** and even **revered** for their wisdom and experience.

In our culture, ageing has become a 'problem' - but only because of the way society has chosen to see old people. We live in an action-orientated world where fast living, fast talking and high achievement count for everything.

Where does that leave someone whose body is slowing down and who is naturally moving towards a more peaceful, inward-looking phase in their life?

It is entirely up to the individual. We don't have to make society's problem with ageing our own. We just need an enlightened attitude and determination to enjoy this next, most interesting phase of life!

Growing old gracefully

As we grow older we find ourselves casting off roles and losing identity in worldly terms. We know many people who feel the same as Gwyn.

You give up your talents and authority and suddenly you feel left with an empty void. If you have been a quick thinker and good organiser you find that now all the younger ones are doing it all without even consulting you or using your experience.

If your health goes you can no longer do what people ask of you. How can you reclaim your sense of inner value when externally you are not given the same recognition as you had before?

Umed and Echhaben Patel

Society tends to class retired people as irrelevant, but we don't have to agree with that, do we? One way of not getting too caught up in our cultural models is to travel to other cultures and witness the immense difference in attitudes to the older generation.

You can travel to India, Thailand, Burma, Malaysia, Polynesia or even as close as France and Spain and see how much the older people are a part of families.

A culture that has no place for its old, wise beings is no culture at all and is said to be lacking in real dignity.

Re-evaluate your worthiness!

It's not a question of having or not having value. It is a question of **changing values** which means no longer attaching them to outer achievements. The way you value yourself and your life in the later years is entirely dependent upon having an attitude that is determined to make life meaningful.

Remember that ageing is a natural process and not something to be dreaded or pushed away.

But I don't feel sixty!

We heard a lovely story recently about someone who had just turned sixty.

He described how he was travelling on a train and had to buy his ticket on the train as he hadn't given himself enough time to get one at the station. It was the first time he had ever asked for a senior citizen's ticket. He said that he felt the same as he did as a young eighteen-year-old when he first asked for an alcoholic drink in a bar, convinced that the bartender wouldn't believe he was old enough. To his amazement the ticket collector just made out the ticket and handed it to him.

'But don't you want to see my identity card?' he asked, sure that he didn't look sixty. The ticket collector just looked at him and said casually, 'Naah!'

How many people feel like this as their body starts to age? Who we are inside is the same all the way through life. 'We' don't age at all, only the body we are travelling around in does. Strange feeling, isn't it?

The best thing is to have a sense of humour about it!

Here's how to know when you are getting old.

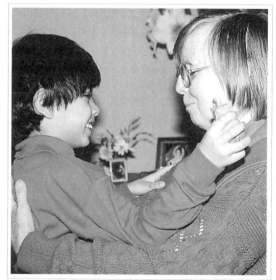

Masum and Jyoti - International Children's Conference

Everything hurts - what doesn't hurt doesn't work
The gleam in your eye is the sun shining on your bifocals
You feel like the morning after but you haven't been anywhere
You get winded playing cards
Your children look middle-aged
You join a health club but don't go
A dripping tap causes an uncontrollable urge
You have all the answers but no-one asks the questions
You look forward to a dull evening

You need glasses to find your glasses
You turn out the light for economy instead of romance
Your knees buckle but your belt won't
Your back goes out more than you do
You put your bra on back to front and it fits better
Your house is too big and your medicine cupboard is not big enough
You sink you teeth into a steak and they stay there
Your birthday cake collapses from the weight of the candles

- Author unknown

The Zest of the Elders

The myth of retirement

For many people retirement seems to be 'the end' but if you have put your life and heart into things that you really enjoy doing in the fifties, then you will have a great opportunity to live a life that you really want to live.

I asked a friend the other day how her friends have responded to retirement. Her answer was simple. 'Most of them have given up doing things they didn't want to do and they are just concentrating on what they love doing.' I asked her if they were happy and she replied, 'Oh yes! But mostly it's the ones who are working for the community who have found a real zest for life and are amongst the happiest people I know.' **If you have found your purpose in life, retirement simply doesn't happen.** You just keep on going. Sounds good to me!

Attitude is everything

Zest comes from enthusiasm and getting excited about what you **can** do. It's an attitude of mind that says, 'Do it now!' instead of waiting until tomorrow. A survey of women in their eighties and nineties found that they were full of zest for life because of their lively attitudes.

They had an enthusiastic enjoyment of the antics of their grandchildren, and a vigorous interest in their 'families' - that meant anything from blood relatives to the whole world. They also had a streak of independence verging on the outrageous, and a well-integrated view of their past. Even factors like healthy food and exercise seemed to be relatively insignificant in keeping these women vital.

When you remain lively, vigorous and fascinated by the fun of life into your eighties and nineties you become ageless because you have tapped into the youthfulness of your own Spirit. Old age gives you the perfect excuse to do exactly what you want to do.

Ageless ageing

A friend gave us this account of shopping with her nearly ninety-year-old father.

We started at the hardware store, where he carefully selected some wood for the new coffee table he is building. Then we looked for wire to complete a picture frame he is making, and after that we visited his publisher to check the progress of a book he has written.

Following this we dropped in at the local wilderness shop to deliver yet more copies of his Bird Calls tape - of which he has sold well over 1,000 copies since producing it four years ago. The staff expressed warm interest in the forthcoming book. I reflected with amusement and love that not everyone taking out their elderly Dad has as much trouble keeping up with him as I do! Even if, as he wryly reflects, his eyes and ears no longer perform as he would wish them to, there's still plenty going on between them!

Frederick Josef Rotblat, a medical physicist and Nobel Peace Prize winner, is a perfect example of someone with real zest for living. Here is an extract from a radio interview he gave.

'What is your short-term goal?' the interviewer asked.
'To rid the world of nuclear weapons. I reckon I can do it in twenty years,' he replied confidently.
There was a period of stunned silence from the interviewer.
'And your long-term goals?' he said eventually.
'To rid the world of war altogether. I won't see it in my lifetime, but I have got to prepare the ground.'
'Don't you feel at 88 you should be passing this work on to others?' said the interviewer.
'Well, sometimes I would agree, but most of the time I don't think so. I am a lot younger on the inside than I look, you know.'

 Life is never over!

Make life interesting!

Reverse the potential for decline!

Acceptance plays a vital role in the process of ageing, as it does at every stage of life. **Accept the changes.** Flow with them and you will be able to reap the best from the age you are in.

Like a trapeze artist in mid-flight between two swings, you have just let go of the old swing - status, income, or perhaps good health - and now you are reaching out. For what?

It can take a while to find something you really want to grab hold of, but any trapeze artist will tell you that it's simply not a good idea to stop in mid-flight! Keep the momentum going! **Ignite your passion** and enthusiasm for life.

Start a huge, foolish project - like Noah! - *Rumi*

The most important thing is to keep your mind alive and excited about your life. Do things you have never done before and go to places you have always wanted to go to. Make your life an adventure!

Winston Churchill became Prime Minister at sixty-five after eight years in the political wilderness.

Agatha Christie re-married in her advanced years and went on to write some of her greatest mysteries.

Catherine Cookson, Britain's best-known authoress, was still writing best-sellers on her ninetieth birthday, having sold well over 90 million books since she was forty-five.

Verdi, Strauss and Sibelius number among many great musicians who did some of their very best work after seventy.

Action plan

What you focus your mind on will determine your experience of life.

✓ Focus on bodily ailments and they will bother you more!

✓ Focus on lost prestige and position in society and you will feel bad!

✓ Focus on appreciation for all your experiences and you will feel grateful for your life.

✓ Focus on **the beauty of life** and you will feel **contented** and **happy.**

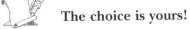 **The choice is yours!**

The Grace of the Elders

Life is beautiful, but in our rushing to achieve we can miss the simple beauty of being here, now, with our life. **Old age is actually a gift from life to us,** not a bane. We are given the opportunity to become still and aware of the life that moves inside us, to fill our hearts with appreciation and gratitude for all the experiences of life.

Old age is about finding inner contentment and inner discovery. It's the age of wonderment and discovering who you really are and what you came here for.

The gifts of old age

In the last few years I have discovered how important it is to keep a close contact with my children - they keep me young! Having four small grandchildren I realise how fortunate I am. They keep me alive, healthy and feeling young. They keep me alive by making me think before I speak because they won't be fobbed off. They keep me healthy by the exercise I get trying to keep up with them and young through the joy and laughter they create.

Playing hide and seek in the pinewoods one day with the children, they called out for a clue as to where I was hiding. I truthfully shouted that I was 'over the hill' and when my husband and I realised what I had said, we both collapsed laughing. Another time on a picnic I was carefully directing everyone over a stream and pointing out slippery places. They all got across safely but I fell in. We laughed so much that I couldn't get out.

- Jean

Years ago, I heard this read out at a cancer conference. For me it captures the charm of how young children view old age.

Grandmothers ...

Grandmothers don't have to do anything but just be there.

Usually they wear glasses and funny underwear and they can take their teeth out as well. They don't have to be clever but only answer questions like, 'Why do dogs hate cats?'

They don't baby-talk like visitors and when they read to us they don't miss bits out or mind if it's the same story over and over again.

Everybody should have a grandmother, especially if you don't have a television.

The lack of physical strength keeps me inactive and often silent.

They call me senile.

Senility is a convenient peg on which to hang non-conformity.

A new set of faculties seems to be coming into operation.

I seem to be waking to a larger world of wonderment.

To catch little glimpses of the immensity and diversity of creation.

More than at any other time of my life I seem to be aware

of the beauties of our spinning planet in the sky above me.

Old age is sharpening my awareness.

- Frances, in a home for the elderly

Near the end of his long life, Mahatma Gandhi observed, 'The less I do, the more seems to happen as a result.' And as he sat calmly in his tiny ashram room, millions rose up around him in a whirlwind that created the greatest non-violent revolution in history.

Whatever your age, when you cease striving to be other than you are, to become 'somebody' better, stronger, cleverer, or more loving - and are simply being - then you become everything and so radiant that everyone wants to be around you.

Every moment is precious

Spending time with Sir George Trevelyan was a revelation to me. It was only three years before he died when I went to visit him in his country home.....

'Such a great man,' I thought to myself as we sat and talked. Here was someone who was known as the Father of the New Age. He was responsible for so much inspiration and had opened the hearts of thousands of people with his lectures and books. Now, he was frail and unable to move easily. His eyes, still bright, would often close as he talked, almost as though the

weight of his eyelids was simply too much for him.

When we went out in the car he took a long time to get in and out. He had to lift his legs up and gently swing them round and across to get them out of the door. But he was radiant. It was so clear to me that the slowness of his body and the painful arthritic joints did not affect the joy that he had identified himself with. Life was still full of pleasure and his appreciation was tangible. Every moment was precious to him, every movement of every leaf significant and the shimmering dance of sunlight on the trees could send him into ecstasy.

But even more beautiful was the stillness around him. He was deeply embedded into the moment. Because time had slowed down so much he was able to taste the flavour of each moment in such a beautiful way. His acceptance of old age, frailty and infirmity was total, and therefore it couldn't touch him.

- *Mansukh*

*If the only prayer you say in the whole of your life is 'thank you' -
that would suffice.*
— Meister Eckhart

Moving into a space of Gratitude

When we are grateful to life for everything it has given us, we will find that we have so much strength and zest. We will not find ourselves feeling depleted or drained by negative or resentful emotions. One colleague of ours was determined to make the most of turning sixty and to eliminate any possibility of becoming depressed about it.

I wanted it to be a celebration of gratitude for my life and my achievements instead of a depressing catalogue of failures! For months beforehand I wrote letters to all the people in my life that I could remember who had ever shared a valuable experience with me. I wanted to thank them for their contribution to my life, however small. I even wrote to one man just because I had known him since I was four years old - and to thank him for that! Some of the letters I had back were quite amazing.

If you are not using your smile,
you are like a man with a million dollars in the bank
without a cheque book.

- Les Giblin

The inner smile meditation

Sit in a position that will be
comfortable for about twenty
minutes.

Close your eyes and take a few
moments to enjoy the opportunity
to sit quietly. Let your breathing
become calm and peaceful.

In this sense of quietness, return to
a time when you were intensely
happy. Let yourself re-live this
experience. Feel the joy and
happiness you felt then. Immerse
yourself in the feelings of that time

M.K. Gandhi - Non-violence and Truth

357

and then allow a gentle smile to come onto your face.

Take this beautiful smile and move it up to your eyes, making them sparkle and shine behind your closed eyelids.

Now carry that smile into your forehead, the back of the head, neck and shoulders, and feel a warm glow developing as it travels around your body. Feel how that smile is melting and softening every part of you.

Let it travel into your heart, filling it with that warmth and then into the lungs, kidneys, liver and stomach. Let it bathe your intestines, your hips and all the way down your legs and into your feet. Then let your smile expand all the way up to your - mouth!

A human being would certainly not grow to seventy or eighty years old if longevity had no meaning.

- Carl Jung

Facing Death and Dying

The sun is rising just where it is setting.
Just as the sun never really sets,
so too does our soul's journey never end.

- Mansukh

When my father was dying I looked after him for many weeks. It was a tender experience for me. It took all the courage in our hearts to face the final departure from each other and now I had accepted his death, as he had. Very soon I would no longer be able to sit and talk with him in the way that I loved and looked forward to with a rich anticipation.

There wasn't anyone else in my life that I could talk to in the same way. He had been my teacher and guide for so many years, not only trained by Gandhi, but a great teacher in his own right. He knew and understood so much about life - and about me. Our relationship was unique and precious and nothing would ever be able to replace it.

But now he was leaving and I felt at ease and very willing to make each precious moment that we had left together count. Just as Gandhi had undertaken a fast to death, we were now feasting on life. We were both totally present, neither of us wishing to be somewhere

Chhaganbhai Patel - 'Dad',1990

else or with someone else, both aware and awake to being together. Each moment seemed to have a substance. He asked. I gave. It was natural. There was an unspoken agreement between us. We shared thoughts and feelings. We smiled and laughed together. Neither of us was afraid. In that time, locked together in a time and space where everything was so real, anything that had ever happened between us in the past became healed. Mischievous to the end, he would joke with me about not taking too long in the toilet just in case his soul flew away.

There was dignity in his dying. For months he had sat quietly on the sofa like a child, full of innocence, yet so obviously in complete control. He knew what was going on and used to talk about death quite openly. He used to tell me that in our tradition it is said that if you die at the right time you heal yourself, if you die in the right way, you heal others, and if your life force leaves the crown of the head at the moment of death, you will have achieved the very highest.

There were so many special moments to remember, like the time an injured white dove arrived outside in the garden. It was unable to fly, and Dad picked it up and nursed it back to health. Eventually it was able to fly round the sitting room all day long until he set it free. Now it was my turn to nurse him so that he could fly away.

During his last moments his breath was laboured and difficult. He opened his eyes and smiled. 'I'm so glad you are here, Mansukh,' he said, his voice almost a whisper. The room seemed to be filled with the deepest peace as though a wave of grace had descended upon us.

I smiled at him, full of gratitude for who he was and the experience of being together, full of love for this man who had meant so much to my own life, full of joy for the journey he was about to make. We smiled at each other and then he closed his eyes and breathed out for the last time. He was gone, like a beautiful wave gently falling back into the ocean.

- Mansukh

Death is natural

Coming from a culture where death is openly displayed and discussed has meant that I have never had any conflict with the process of dying. As a very young boy I witnessed so many scenes of illness, disease and death that now it is completely natural to me.

In a country like India where life and death co-exist quite happily, you will not encounter the fear of death that is predominant in our Western civilisation. Dead bodies are openly carried through the streets wrapped only in a thin muslin cloth and displayed on a funeral pyre for all to see.

In the so-called 'civilised' countries of the world death is hidden away behind closed doors, not discussed or even thought about until the day it 'happens'. When it does, it becomes a subject of fear and distrust. Young people are often so shocked when out of the blue they find themselves having to attend the funeral of someone close to them.

Without any previous experience, they find themselves unable to cope because no-one has ever taught them how to deal with death.
This attitude reminds me of the way little children cover their faces with their hands when they play hide and seek and really believe that no-one can see them. If we don't look at death - it isn't there!

Eurowalk 2000 - India 1997

Let children walk with nature,
let them see the beautiful blendings and communions of death and life,
their joyous inseparable unity, as taught in woods and meadows,
plains and mountains and streams of our blessed star,
and they will learn that death is stingless indeed,
and as beautiful as life,
and that the grave has no victory,
for it never fights.
All is divine harmony.

- John Muir,
father of American Nature Conservation

Awakening to Dying

Death is part of the journey of life and not 'a mistake' or something to be ignored. In fact death contains the very *secret of life* and can awaken us to that mystery.

My father loved to tell stories to illustrate a point and one of his favourites told of a man who was walking along the road at twilight. All of a sudden he froze. There in front of him, poised to strike, was a deadly snake.

He recoiled in horror, as terror took hold of him. Then, as his eyes became more focussed, he realised it wasn't a snake at all, but just a curled-up piece of vine.

Dad explained that the man's problem wasn't legitimate because he had only projected the image of a snake onto the vine.
It wasn't really there. In the same way, we can project our fear and trepidation onto death but **it's not legitimate** and the only solution is to **see it as it really is.**

When we can truly see and understand that there is **nothing to fear,** we

become released from the illegitimate 'problem'.

Death and dying offer us a real chance to understand what our life is all about and if it's our own death that we are facing then it's our last chance to discover **why we are alive!**

370

For what is it to die but to stand naked in the wind
and to melt into the sun?
And what is it to cease breathing
but to free the breath from its restless tides,
that it may rise and expand and seek God unencumbered?
Only when you drink from the river of silence shall you indeed sing.
And when you have reached the mountain top,
then you shall begin to climb.
And when the earth shall claim your limbs,
then shall you truly dance.

- *Kahlil Gibran*

371

What is the fear of death all about?

Death has always been portrayed in a way that evokes fear within us and the ghastly skeletal figure of 'The Grim Reaper' hasn't helped at all! Even in the Indian tradition where death is accepted as natural, the God of Death, Lord Yama, is said to appear as a big black figure riding on a bull to steal our souls away.

In our minds we tend to cling to these images rather than the lighter, more ethereal Christian idea of smiling angels all around us floating on clouds of golden light. I wonder why we prefer to attach the experience of death to an image that is terrifying?

Death has been abused by religions and used to create a fear of 'hell and damnation' if we don't live our lives in the right way. As a result many people grow up in fear of the terrible things that are going to happen 'at the end'.

Where am I going to?

Because we don't know, we can imagine all sorts of frightening things, like waking up on another planet where we don't recognise anybody and can't speak the language. Death appears to be the end of everything we hold dear. The familiar and the known are going to be taken away for ever and we may imagine we are going to feel lost, alone and bewildered.

Perhaps that is why people who have had near-death experiences and 'glimpsed the beyond' seem to lose their fear of death. They have discovered that death is not frightening or horrible but rather filled with beauty, serenity and love. For this reason it's a good idea to read books about other people's 'brushes with death' which can help to allay our fears of the unknown.

When a Beloved one is Dying

What can you do to help someone to make their final journey towards death? We, like Mother Teresa, believe that everyone deserves to die with dignity and a feeling of being unconditionally loved. Shirley, a close friend and colleague of ours, recently discovered the power of unconditional love when she nursed her sister as she was dying.

It is an incredible gift to be with someone when they die. I learned, perhaps for the very first time, what it feels like to love unconditionally, simply because there wasn't anything else I could do.

Every minute of the day was dedicated to trying to make something meaningful of however long she had left. It was an unexpected gift for me, because I hadn't realised before how close we were and what she really meant to me.

Something told me that if I could care for her in the right way, it would make such a difference to the way she died. I did everything I could to love her, care for her, and create a peaceful atmosphere, setting the scene for the last weeks of her life and not pushing away the whole experience.

Eurowalk 2000 - Northern India - River Yamuna, Vrindaban

375

Shona, another very close friend of ours recently nursed her mother who was dying of cancer and found it to be an awakening experience. She had many realisations and insights into the meaning of life. This is her story.

They say that the eighth wonder of the world is that people don't or won't believe that they will ever die. And it's true! Somehow you never believe that someone you love will one day go away. That's why it hurts so much when it happens. You are just unprepared. As Mum's condition deteriorated I think everyone in the family went through every possible emotion.

Sometimes I felt so desperate and helpless and often the only thing that kept me going was my diary. I wrote everything down each day, each experience, every pain and joy, and kept it up no matter what I was feeling. Somehow it helped me when there was no-one else to turn to and now I treasure it because it is so tangible. It has become the most incredible record of my love for my mother.

Diary - June 30th

I watch the love between Mum and Dad grow more and more tender each day. Oh, how I wish it did not have to take such an immense explosion as death to wake people up to life! The time should always be NOW to tell people how much you love them.

I used to sit next to my mother and really, really appreciate her. Tears would come into my eyes as I held her hands and looked at every line and crease, their shape, colour and texture and think about all the hard work she had done with them. When she finally died it helped so much to know that I had done everything I could for her. Something inside me felt full and free from regrets.

Diary - September 19th

I went to the funeral parlour to see Mum for the last time before her burial. I think the thing that struck me most was that there was such a hollow, empty feeling about her body. I realise with such deep certainty that there **must** be a soul to give it life. We are all souls clothed with bodies. We must learn to use them wisely.

And her conclusion.....
Death really is an amazing thing. It blows people wide open. Even Dad said yesterday, 'Words take on a whole new meaning.' Whenever we lose our perspective or fall back into unhelpful negative patterns, we need to reflect on death and impermanence. It will shake us back into truth.

Nothing is solid or lasting and everything changes.
Even our thoughts are unpredictable!
The only thing we have is this moment NOW.
And life is NOW and what we do in the NOW.

Shona's Mother

Nursing a beloved one who is dying

This is the most precious time for both of you and in order to make it special, there are six crucial things that you must do.

Touch - Use the power of human touch, which is a vital source of comfort and healing. Sick people long to be touched and massaging their feet and hands brings a great sense of comfort and ability to relax. If you can hold them in your arms or stroke their hair it will mean so much to them.

Patience - Try to approach the situation with a great deal of patience. Give yourself time and decide to put everything else on hold and attend to this person who is dying. They may go at any moment, or it may take a long time for them to make their transition, so it's important to be **very patient.**

Understanding - Dying brings up a lot of emotions that may have been suppressed and need to come to the surface to be released. You will need to help them through this process with a lot of understanding. They may feel angry, frightened or sad and it's important to understand that they are losing everything they hold dear all at once as they approach death: their material possessions, their body, their faculties, as well as leaving behind the people they love.

They may well be afraid and need constant reassurance. Fear of death can make people aggressive or even violent at times. Try not to judge them by their emotions. If the dying person feels unconditionally loved and accepted no matter what they are expressing, they will slowly be able to let go and accept themselves and their feelings.

But I'm not a saint!
If their behaviour is unreasonable, it helps to focus on their inner goodness! Consciously think of them as they are at their very best and associate them with that state.

Unconditional Love - This is more important than anything else and is the most powerful force on earth. Try to keep your heart wide open to them and the situation as a whole and you will experience that love can heal anything.

Process and accept your own fears -
The patient's fears about dying can be disturbing and bring up your own fear of death. Look at your fears honestly and ask yourself what they might be. It could be fear of loss, separation, suffering and pain, indignity, rejection or losing control.

If you can confront your own fears you will find you will feel much more compassionate and able to cope with the fears of others.

Action plan

◆ Think about your fear.

◆ Breathe it in and then out through the crown of your head and into a space of white light about an arm's length above your head.

◆ See the situation change and the fear transform itself.

◆ Breathe it back down through the crown into your heart and then out from the heart to a space in front of you. Do this three times.

Unfinished business

The process of dying involves making peace with our life and healing the past. If a person feels incomplete with unresolved issues it may prevent them from letting go. The soul knows when the process is complete and can be released.

During the time after my mother's death, Dad seemed to become very deeply settled into his life. He was preparing to pass on, and he knew there were certain things he had to do first. He had to cast a net out into the world to try to catch hold of any unfinished business.

He began to wake up very early in the morning when it was still dark and to go outside and gaze at the stars, sometimes for hours. I often used to watch him looking intently at the clouds and smiling to himself as he sipped his tea, almost as though they were talking to him and he was reading their messages.

One day out of the blue he announced, 'It's time to go to India, and you must make time to come as well, Mansukh. It will be very important for you.' Immediately he began his preparations, his eyes took on a distant look, as though he was already there.

As soon as we arrived in Hansapur, the village where he was born and grew up, he received a message that a very special person wanted to see him. 'Yes, I know,' he said simply, 'I am ready.' It was a friend he had known fifty-five years before as a young boy. He and a small band of friends had studied under a spiritual teacher at that time and the depth of the experience they shared had created a deep bond between them all. The last of these friends was still alive and waiting to see Dad before he passed away.

When we arrived at his little hut we found an old man lying on a rough pallet above the soft earthen floor. A dim oil lamp burned in

386

Dad's friend , India 1988

the corner and an old wooden stick leaned against the bed. A few white clothes hung on a nail on the wall. Knowing that he was dying he had stopped eating for weeks before, taking only a few drops of water from time to time.

Both of them appeared to have the same intensity in their eyes. They were so alike - the same look, the same smile - except one was lying down and the other standing. The dying man reached up and pulled Dad close to him by his beads as a rush of love and feeling passed between them. 'I knew you would come,' he said as they began to share sixty years of tears. After embracing each other for more than ten minutes the old man looked up at me and held on to my hand. 'You have a beautiful son,' he said to Dad, 'and you have trained him well.' Dad just nodded.

The room seemed alive, full of power and vibrancy as these two giants of an ancient tradition exchanged gestures, glances and words. They talked about their childhood together, reminiscing quietly about their shared adventures.

Finally the old man sighed deeply and said, 'Don't forget to bless my smoke, Chhaganbhai.' My father smiled knowingly. He was referring to his journey towards death.

How could he possibly have known that Dad would come from so far away? We had no idea what power had brought them together again after so long, but the sight of those two great patriarchs rejoined in a fusion of brotherhood is one I will never forget.

- Mansukh

Relationships need to be resolved and healed. The dying person needs to forgive and feel forgiven, and to say what needs to be said to all their loved ones. Shirley describes how the need to 'complete' gave her dying sister new life.

She had been bedridden for weeks, unable to move at all and it used to take ages just to get her to the toilet. One day, she suddenly became excited, indicating that she wanted to go into the garden. We were amazed at this sudden burst of energy, as for many weeks she had been afraid to even go near the outside door.

We followed her outside and all the way to the garden shed. I rushed to get the key as soon as I realised what she wanted to do. It was the place where her husband had spent many happy hours repairing furniture. We waited, holding our breath to see what was going to happen.

Sue Turner - Maristowe

All his tools were there and she gently and lovingly moved towards them and started to place her hand on each one of them until she had touched them all. She was saying a most intimate goodbye to him and all her memories.

We stood there quietly watching her, as tears rolled down our cheeks.

The most powerful aspect of my sister's death for me occurred after she had died. We laid her out in a beautiful nightdress and put her on the sofa in the sitting room in full view of everyone. Initially people were very shocked when they saw her there, expecting her to have been 'taken away'. It didn't take very long before they got used to it, however, and it felt quite special because it made us all face the fact that she was actually dead.

Often people's fear of the reality of death can create a kind of contraction in the atmosphere, but when you find yourself having to face the truth of the situation something seems to expand around you. The room filled with the most beautiful peace that made you want to be there and it made us all realise that death is not the end. We were all forced to acknowledge her.

It felt quite amazing and perfectly natural.

- Shirley

Do not stand at my grave and weep,
I am not there, I do not sleep.
I am a thousand winds that blow,
I am the diamond glints on snow.
I am the sunlight on ripened grain,
I am the gentle autumn rain.
When you awaken in the morning's hush,
I am the uplifting rush
of quiet birds in circled flight.
I am the soft stars that shine at night.
Do not stand at my grave and cry,
I am not there, I did not die.

- Anon

Preparing Yourself for Death

In the Eastern traditions it has always been upheld that life is a preparation for the moment of death. It is said that we should always keep life on one shoulder and death on the other, in constant awareness of our mortality, never taking for granted that we will be alive tomorrow. This is portrayed in the story of the Mahabharata.

Yudhisthira, the eldest of the Pandava brothers, one day opened the door to a sick man who asked for a special kind of food. Yudhisthira apologised to the man for the fact that he could not help him, but promised that if he returned the next day he would make sure that he could. Bhima, his younger brother, began to laugh out loud, and immediately started ringing a huge bell, calling all the brothers together.

'Listen to this!' he said excitedly. 'Today, right here in our very midst I have heard something I thought I would never hear!'

The brothers looked on in amazement. 'What on earth is it, Bhima?' they asked.

'With my very own ears,' he said, gesticulating wildly, 'I have heard Yudhisthira say that he will be here tomorrow!'

The message is clear that we must all try to live fully,
in deep appreciation of the gifts that life is giving,
never assuming life will last forever.

Chernobyl children - Snowdon Lodge, North Wales

1 Gratitude

Now is the time to appreciate and be thankful for everything that life has given you, and everyone in your life. Now is the time to say, 'I love you,' to people. John is a friend of ours who, in his seventies, told us about his experience of living close to death.

_____

I am now living one day at a time and I never expect to wake up in the morning. But I always feel so grateful when I do! Consequently, everything has begun to take on a sense of wonder for me.

Recently I had a heart scan in which I could see my own heart pumping. I found it hard to believe that it had always been there, keeping me alive but I had never really even thought about it before. I suddenly felt a great wave of appreciation for this little organ that had been sustaining my life for seventy years. 'My God!' I realised, 'I am alive! It's a miracle!'

2 Generosity

There is an old spiritual law that says, 'Always leave this world giving because generosity can turn sinners into saints!' It refers to the importance of keeping the energy of material resources flowing, so that they do not stagnate. The reason is because stagnation is not a good thing to leave behind you. Let things flow freely now to help people who are in need.

My father always told me that whatever you do in your life, it is important to make sure that it benefits seven future generations. An example he gave was planting a forest of mango trees.

It is also a very good idea to use some money to help people who cannot say, 'thank you', like the children in Bosnia or Chernobyl.

I heard a story recently about a football coach in the United States who was dying of a crippling cancer. He left a legacy of hope behind him.

He developed cancer of the spine and had only ten months left to live. Determined to make a difference with the remainder of his life he called a meeting with all the top businessmen and multi-millionaires in America.

Hobbling in on crutches, hardly able to walk, he persuaded them to set up a trust to help people with cancer. 'If a child comes to you with cancer in five years' time, I want you to tell him that you can cure him!' he said.
'Not only that, I believe that you will be able to do it.'

Spurred on by his words and his passionate belief, they went on to raise $3 billion for cancer research.

3 *Forgiveness*

Forgiveness is another form of generosity and frees a lot of energy that may have been stuck for a very long time. If anyone has hurt you in your life, now is the time to **forgive** and **let go.**

There was once a man who had a very difficult son. He was disobedient, unruly and bad-mannered, never helping out or considering anyone else's needs. In desperation, he asked his brother, who was a holy man, to come and talk to him and 'sort him out'.

The boy's old uncle dutifully came, but he just stayed in his room and prayed all night, not saying a word to the son. In the morning he simply got up and prepared to leave. His brother couldn't understand why he hadn't approached his son in any way, and neither could the son, who had been expecting a 'lecture'.

As he was leaving, he asked the boy to tie his shoe-laces for him. The boy knelt down at his feet and as he did so, he felt drops of water falling on his head. He looked up and saw that the old man was crying.

'What is it, Uncle?' he asked him in amazement. 'Why are you crying?'

'I am so grateful that you are tying my shoe-laces,' he said, 'because you are probably the last person who will ever do it for me, as I am dying.'

He left the house without saying anything else and the young boy became completely transformed from that moment.

Action plan - Forgive Yourself

It's important to know that divinity does not forgive - simply because it does not condemn. So it is also very important to **forgive yourself** for anything you may have done in your life that you may find unforgivable.

The following exercise is a practice which will wipe the slate clean and has the power to ensure that you die with serenity.

♦   Make sure you are sitting comfortably and feeling relaxed. Begin by invoking the presence of a saint or holy person that you feel close to. See the saint as a being of light. If you do not have an affinity with any spiritual figure, simply imagine a form of pure, golden light in front of you.

♦   Imagine your consciousness as a point of light in your heart centre which flashes out from you and into the light in front of you. Let it dissolve and merge into it.

◆ Address it in this way.

**Through the power of light that streams through you
may all my negative thoughts and actions
be purified and removed.
May I know that I am forgiven
for any harm I may have thought or done.
May I die a good and peaceful death.
Through my death, may I be able to benefit other people
whether living or dead.**

◆ Now imagine rays of golden light pouring from the heart of light towards you. As it touches you, you become immersed in light and are completely cleansed and purified.

Action plan - preparing for death.

If you were going to die tomorrow..........how would you like to be remembered?

Imagine you have just died and are lying in your coffin which is open. All your friends and relatives are standing around you in a circle holding hands. They are each going to say something about what you have meant to them and what you have contributed to their lives and to the world.

What would they say ....? What would you **like** them to say?

 What actions could you take today to make sure you are remembered in this way?

◆ Choose one of the poems in this chapter that really means
    something to you and make a commitment to read it every day.

◆ Attend the funeral of someone you don't know to get used to
    the feeling of death without any association of bereavement.

◆ Go to a graveyard. Touch the gate and walk away. Why?
    Because very few people go there and walk away alive!

You would know the secret of death.
But how shall you find it unless you seek it in the heart of life?
The owl whose night-bound eyes are blind unto the day
cannot unveil the mystery of light.
If you would indeed behold the spirit of death,
open your heart wide unto the body of life.
For life and death are one,
even as the river and the sea are one.

- Kahlil Gibran

Where Does Life End and Death Begin?

Does the sunrise start with the first rays of the sun? When **exactly** do we breathe in and out? When does life begin? Is it conception? Birth? The first cry? Does childhood end on a certain day at a certain time and the teenage years begin?

In fact, there simply isn't a place or time where life ends and death begins, just as there isn't a place where one stage of life ends and another begins. Such a fine timing **simply doesn't exist.** Life and death overlap and are intermingled like two chromosomes entwined around each other.

People think death only represents about 3% of the experience of life and is something that comes like a blow 'at the end'. But life and death are living **side by side** in every moment in a perfectly equal relationship.

407

Life and death reflect two sides of the same consciousness just like night and day are two aspects of the sun's influence, one depending on the other for its existence and each an inseparable and integral part of the other.

Renewal must take place

In nature, death and renewal are perfectly intertwined and always taking place. Leaves fall from the trees and are renewed in the spring. Some insects are born in the morning only to die at night. All around us there is a continuous cycle of death and renewal.

Human beings, however, are one of the few species that don't give themselves a chance to renew every year. Mother Nature must have anticipated this trait because she has given us a great secret.

We have the ability to renew ourselves constantly through our **breath**.

Can death really be living by the side of life?

Our breath is the key to the mystery of life and death for in every inbreath life is born and in every outbreath life is transformed into death, just as the first breath that enters a baby's body heralds its life and the last breath, whether it is a few days, weeks or years later, brings the end of that life. The French even call sleep 'La Petite Mort' or 'Little Death'.

Just as we live during the day and die at night when we are asleep, birth and death are happening to us *all the time*. Every heartbeat and space between, constitutes a birth and death. **Death is the renewal of a living process.**

If we can really understand and assimilate this truth, we will begin to get close to the explosive potential that life and death bring to us here, now, in every living moment.

Becoming aware of the proximity of death in every moment offers us a great freedom from the fear of death.

The potential exists to become perfectly happy about and excited by this very natural process.

We don't have to wait until we are old and rickety for death to happen to us. It's happening now!

Just as we cannot breathe in without breathing out, so we cannot be reborn without dying.

On the edge of life and death

A cry goes out into the East African night sky as a new life enters the world.

It's touch and go as to whether the baby will live or not. There are complications, and living in the bush they are not able to get to a hospital. The midwife doesn't hold out much hope.

The young English couple hold on to their child, constantly massaging his little arms and legs and rubbing the sternum, all the time willing him to live.

All night long as his exhausted wife sleeps, the father keeps his eyes fixed on his tiny son's chest and abdomen, watching the rising and falling, rising and falling, rising and falling. Every now and again he pushes his little legs backwards and forwards to make sure he keeps breathing.

411

He never takes his eyes off the baby's chest for a single moment until morning when the midwife comes and assures them that yes, this baby is going to make it!

Returning to England many years later, someone asked him what his most lasting impression had been amidst all the colour and excitement of African life.

'The rising and falling of my son's chest,' he said simply. 'It was the most precious time in my life, because it made me realise what life is really all about.'

 The only thing that really matters is the in-breath and the out-breath!

And life is eternal
And love is immortal
And death is only an horizon
And an horizon is nothing
save the limit of our sight.

**Now you have all the knowledge and tools you need to live your life
fully in every moment. Please don't wait till you die to understand the
power of life.**

Life is a precious gift,
so take it into your own hands and live it now!

We call them miracle points

Appendix

   When you experience pain, that particular part of your body is
   sending you a message. These tables will help you discover
   what this message is. Use the corresponding miracle
   affirmations to build positive thought patterns to re-establish
   health in mind and body.

A Guide to the Major Life Transition Points

Transition Age	What is happening to me?	Area to focus on during this period	Qualities available to help us
Birth	*Potential*	*Objects of the world*	*Wonderment Playfulness Laughter*
11-14	*Emergence*	*Training the physical body and emotions*	*Confidence Discovery Excitement*
19-21	*Development*	*Self-expression and communication*	*Courage Exploration Intimacy*
27-32	*Choice*	*Building your life and controlling the mind*	*Responsibility Energy Work*

A Guide to the Major Life Transition Points

Transition Age	What is happening to me?	Area to focus on during this period	Qualities available to help us
38-42	*Re-evaluation*	*Relationship with self and others*	*Healing Maturity Awakening*
48-52	*Expansion*	*Giving to others*	*Generosity Freedom Adventure*
58-62	*Internalisation*	*Passing on wisdom*	*Wisdom Gratitude Contentment*
Death	*Release*	*Dealing with unfinished business*	*Stillness Peace*

A Guide to Your Body's Messages

Organ	Emotion / Negative Tendency	Miracle Affirmation
Heart	*Denial of Self-Love*	*I love myself unconditionally.*
Liver	*Anger / Jealousy*	*There is an abundance of love in the universe - I am open to receive.*
Gall Bladder	*Bitterness / Resentment*	*I forgive the past and let go.*
Kidneys	*Fear / Anxiety*	*I am totally safe. Life is on my side.*
Lungs	*Grief / Sadness*	*I accept everything as it is and give generously to the world.*
Spleen	*Lack of self-trust*	*I trust in myself totally.*

A Guide to Your Body's Messages

Organ	Emotion / Negative Tendency	Miracle Affirmation
Bladder	*Worry/Anxiety*	*I let go of all worries and trust in the Universe.*
Pancreas	*Lack of appreciation of life*	*I open to life and appreciate all its gifts.*
Stomach, Intestines	*Inability to digest life*	*I absorb life fully and completely.*
Skin	*Negative feelings about oneself*	*I feel the joy of my spirit always.*
Central Nervous System	*Agitated mind*	*Every breath I take I breathe in calm.*
Blood	*Denial of the river of joy*	*I allow the river of joy to flow through me freely.*

A Guide to Your Body's Messages

Part of Body	Thought Pattern / Negative Tendency	Miracle Affirmation
Head	*Lack of self-worth*	*I am beautiful, I accept myself as I am.*
Hair	*Feeling of weakness against life's challenges*	*I have the strength within me to do anything I need to do.*
Ears	*Inability to listen to life*	*I open to what life is telling me.*
Eyes	*Inability to see life as it is*	*I accept life, my present and my future.*
Neck	*Inflexibility in our thinking*	*I am totally flexible in the way life presents itself to me.*
Throat	*Inability to express oneself*	*I express myself fully and completely.*

A Guide to Your Body's Messages

Part of Body	Thought Pattern / Negative Tendency	Miracle Affirmation
Arms	*Inability to embrace life*	*I embrace life totally.*
Hands	*Inability to handle life skilfully*	*I handle life with gentleness and ease.*
Back	*Feeling of being unsupported by life*	*The universe supports me in everything that I do.*
Hips, Legs	*Fear to move forward in life*	*I walk on fearlessly, knowing that only the best is before me.*
Feet	*Inability to understand life*	*I allow myself to stand under life to open to what life is showing me.*
Mouth	*Inability to receive new ideas*	*I take nourishment from all that life is offering me.*

Basic Foot Massage

A thorough foot massage is one of the best ways of revitalising yourself.
The body's circulation is stimulated and the relaxation response is
activated. Every organ and part of the body is represented in the feet,
so by massaging them you are massaging the whole body.

Begin by soaking the feet in a bowl of warm to hot water which has had
a few drops of fresh ginger juice added to it. After 10-15 minutes, dry
the feet and massage deeply with sesame oil. Taking one foot at a time,
use firm pressure to knead the soles and to work around the heels and
ankles. Moving to the front of the foot, use your thumbs to press
between the toes and along the webbing towards the ankles. This
action stimulates the lymphatic drainage process. Conclude your foot
massage by squeezing and pressing each toe in turn, stimulating the
circulation and flow of electromagnetic energy. Now repeat for the
other foot. A good, basic foot massage should take you about 15-20
minutes.

Basic foot massage is an excellent preparation for the activation of your 'miracle points'.

Massaging using the Miracle Points

Now you may select some of the Miracle Points from the diagram overleaf as appropriate.

To activate the Miracle Points, apply a firm pressure with the thumb for up to 20 seconds at a time on the selected point. Repeat this seven times, gradually increasing the pressure.

Miracle Points

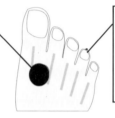

Stress Point
On the web between the 1st & 2nd toes, 2 thumb widths from the margin of the web. Calms the mind, releases irritability and frustration. Good for PMT. Alleviates migraine headaches, muscle cramp and spasms.

Calming Point
Squeeze the tip of the 4th toe. This point is for asthma, headaches and inflammation of the throat.

Fatigue Point
Three thumb widths directly above the vertex of the inner ankle bone, on the edge of the shin bone.
Good for tiredness, regulates menstrual cycle and alleviates menstrual pain. CAUTION - do not use during pregnancy.

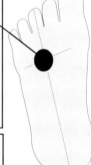

Crisis Coping Point
Draw an imaginary line on the sole of your foot from the tip of your middle toe to your heel, then another line across the ball of your foot. The point is located at the place where these two lines meet. Calms the mind and dissolves extreme fear and anxiety.

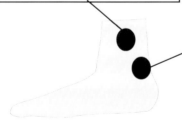

Energisation Point
Half way between the Achilles tendon and the inside ankle bone. Strengthens the lower back and knees. Good for chronic tiredness.

427

Index of Movement and Visualisation Techniques

Index of Movement and Visualisation Techniques

Although the techniques in these lists appear within particular ages of life, they are relevant for every age.

Author's note

To the best of our knowledge all the stories in this book are true.

We have used the actual names of the people in the stories whenever they have given us permission to do so. Despite exhaustive enquiries we were unable to contact two of the people mentioned but found their stories so inspiring we decided to take a leap of faith and include them. If you recognise your story and would like to contact us we would be delighted to hear from you.

Biographies

Mansukh Patel, Ph.D., D.O.

Dr Mansukh Patel is a remarkable man. He is a philosopher, scientist, osteopath, author and teacher.

Born in the Kenyan Rift Valley in 1955, his early upbringing and education were based on the traditional Gandhian philosophy of his parents as well as the indigenous principles of the local Masai villagers with whom he had close contact. Based on timeless wisdom, this knowledge came naturally to him and acted as a foundation stone on which all the later achievements of his life were to stand.

Arriving in the UK at the age of twelve, Mansukh was also able to absorb all the essential qualities of Western culture and education. He went on to study biochemistry and cancer toxicology, later qualifying as an osteopath. A founder member of the Life Foundation School of Therapeutics, he became well-known and much sought-after for his skills in teaching people techniques for living a happy, creative and fulfilling life.

Since 1985 he has been walking to share his message and wisdom with the world. Eurowalk 2000 has taken him not only all around the UK and also to countries such as Bosnia, Croatia, Poland, Ireland and the Netherlands where his techniques for managing and overcoming crisis have always been received with great enthusiasm.

Dr Patel has produced seven books, including *Face to Face with Life* and the best-selling *The Dance Between Joy and Pain,* as well as more than twenty video and audio tapes on topics such as self-confidence and self-esteem, meditation, yoga and harmonious relationships. Three television documentaries have been made about his work.

When he is not walking and teaching he lives in North Wales with his wife and three children.

Helena Waters, M.B.B.S., M.R.C.Psych., M.Sc., D.P.M.

Born in 1947, Dr Waters was brought up and educated in Australia. After graduating from medical school in Adelaide, she came to the UK where she practised psychiatry for ten years.

Wishing to apply the knowledge and skills she had accumulated during this time she branched out into the field of management training. She became well-known for introducing management training for doctors in the N.H.S. As she adopted a more holistic approach to health care, this became an increasingly important feature of her work and she was soon pioneering work, both within and outside the N.H.S., to bridge the gap between orthodox and holistic practice.

Never one to shy away from embracing change and sharing her own empirically-gained knowledge with others, Dr Waters has been instrumental in developing workshops in 'Women's Health Matters'.

In these she empowers women to use the menopause as a stepping stone to greater achievement. As part of the Eurowalk 2000 project she has travelled and taught extensively throughout the UK, the Netherlands, Poland and the Czech Republic.

Dr Waters has produced several audio cassettes on stress management and holistic solutions to women's health issues.

Acknowledgements

This book owes its entire existence to Eurowalk 2000. It contains the cream and essence of our walk experience.

The list of all those that we would like to extend our thanks to is endless. They have, each one, enriched our lives and expanded our vision for a better world. The stories that we have heard, the inspirations and contributions that we have received and the support that we have been given throughout Bosnia, the Netherlands, Germany, Poland, Ireland and the UK have been incredible. This book is a gift from all of them to all of us and is an inspiration of the highest merit.

In particular we would like to thank Sally Langford, Paul Clarke and Andrew Wells who have spent many months compiling, researching and writing. A special thank you to Regina Doerstel for her cover design and for page-setting and book design. To Barbara Wood and Jane Clapham for endless hours of creative typesetting and correction. To Nanna Coppens, Chris Ion, John Scard and Jeff Cushing, we extend our

our deepest thanks for their skill in illustration. To David Manders and Suzie Wolff for several of the amazing photographs and to Kate Couldwell, Gwyneth Clapham, Ruth Boaler and Jessica Scard for the hours of patient, painstaking proofreading.

Special thanks to Jane Patel, John Jones, Gordon Turner, Rosemary McIntyre, Chris Barrington, Annie Jones and Rita Goswami for all their enthusiasm, creative ideas, encouragement, support and advice.
To all our colleagues at the Life Foundation School of Therapeutics who have supported our journeys and pilgrimages - without whom this work would not have been possible.

Thanks to our special friend, Jan de Vries, for his sincere foreword and last, but not least, we thank Mahatma Gandhi, St Francis, Echaben and Chhaganbhai Patel (Mansukh's parents) for their inspiration and guidance by example.

BELIEVE IN YOURSELF
Dr Mansukh Patel
On this best selling tape, Dr Mansukh Patel presents in simple language extraordinary concepts for self-esteem. Would you like to build relationships that satisfy you? Would you like to learn practical ways to achieve a strong personality? This tape tells you how. It also includes a 5 minute introspection technique for turning repeated failures into triumphs.

FACE TO FACE WITH LIFE
Dr Mansukh Patel and John Jones
'Face to Face with Life' is a powerful handbook for successful living...it is also a miraculous true story. Containing over a hundred breakthrough techniques to increase self-esteem, improve relationships and develop inner calm. Meanwhile, enjoy the gripping story of a group of University students who became the pioneers of the Life Foundation, and who have brought real happiness into thousands of lives world-wide. *This popular book is now available in Dutch from Ankh Hermes.*

438

CELEBRATING MENOPAUSE

Dr Helena Waters & Liz Rowan SRN

Balancing ourselves and our hormones - naturally! Celebrate this successful approach to the 'Change of life' and learn everything you've always wanted to know about positive approaches to hormone health and natural, safe alternatives to HRT. Gentle movements and relaxation exercises are included to help with this process.

(Part 2 of the Menopause Series)

STRESS MANAGEMENT

Dr Helena Waters & Anita Goswami

When we have least time to relax is when we need it most! Stress affects our work, health and relationships and can become difficult to control - so learn how to break the pattern and control the stress before it controls you! This tape also includes simple yet effective techniques to incorporate into your daily routine.

439

OVERCOMING EMOTIONAL PAIN

Dr Mansukh Patel

Fear, anger and grief are probably the three most destructive emotions that we can experience. Mansukh shares with you practical, flowing movements, developed from 'The Dance Between Joy and Pain', which will transform these emotions. These techniques have been used successfully with top personnel from the United Nations High Commission for Refugees in Bosnia.

THE DANCE BETWEEN JOY AND PAIN

Dr Mansukh Patel & Rita Goswami

This handbook has become a source of inspiration and reference for thousands of people since it was first published in 1995. It is a manual for mastering all the negative emotions we experience, from anger and grief to jealousy and loneliness. Practical movements, breathing exercises and hand gestures combine to transform emotions into positive tools to enrich every aspect of life. *Now in its fourth reprint, 'The Dance Between Joy and Pain' is available in Dutch and is currently being translated into French and Russian.*

The Dance Between Joy and Pain.

This little book offers you ways to use the strength of your emotions - whether joyful or painful - to empower your life. Inspirational reading,

Erika Harvey, Editor Here's Health.

440

SURYA NAMASKAR

Annie Jones & Dr Mansukh Patel

The traditional movements of the Sun Sequence are brought to you complete with powerful mantras, making it ideal to balance the metabolism and banish fatigue. Side B of the tape contains the energising 'Great Candle Flame' relaxation, guided by Dr Mansukh Patel to refresh body and mind.

THE IMMORTALITY SEQUENCE

Rita Goswami

This tape combines movement and instruction. Its purpose - to empower the very highest part of yourself. It works! This series of gentle exercises and affirmations will attune your Body, Heart and Mind to allow your inherent strength to become a living reality in your life. Watch your self esteem grow, and your personal and professional relationships flourish.

Other Tape Titles Available -

from the Life Foundation School of Therapeutics

Sound and Mantra
Love Yourself
Call of the Flute
Healing Difficult Relationships
Six Steps to Making Successful Relationships
Law of Abundant Energy
Effective Time and Energy Management
Effortless Concentration
The Heart of the Matter
Stretch for Health
Back Pain Relief
Meditations for Inner Strength

Please phone or write for a full colour catalogue. We look forward to hearing from you.

L.F.S.T.,   Maristowe House, Dover St, Bilston, W.Mids WV14 6AL, UK
Tel (+44) 01902 409164, Fax 497362, Email lfst@ukemail.com

Letter to the Reader

I would like to thank you for purchasing and reading this copy of *Crisis and the Miracle of Love*. I know that the stories, insights and techniques will have helped you to gain greater perspective, happiness and fulfilment in your life.

One of the things that we find most valuable in our work is sharing real-life success stories. We would like to give you the opportunity to send in your own 'miracle points' - your rich, magical, heroic, heart-opening, even extraordinary experiences. With your permission we might use them in further publications to help inspire and uplift the lives of others.

Furthermore, if you encounter anything unusual or miraculous as a result of reading this book, we would be delighted to hear from you. Please send your stories to me at: Maristowe House, Dover Street, Bilston, West Midlands, WV14 6AL. For your effort we would love to send you a special surprise gift. Thank you for your care and concern. I look forward to hearing from you.

- Dr Helena Waters

For Your Personal Notes

For Your Personal Notes